Oranges From Dominic's Tree

Selected Poems by Dominican Friars, Sisters and Laity

Compiled and introduced
by
Matthew Powell, O.P.

NEW PRIORY PRESS
EXPLORING THE DOMINICAN VISION

Copyright © 2014 by the Dominican Province of St. Albert the Great (U.S.A.) All rights reserved. Published by New Priory Press, 1910 South Ashland Avenue, Chicago, IL 60608-2903
NewPrioryPress.com

Dedicated to

George Leonard Cochran, O.P.

1928 - 2013

Priest, Teacher, Poet and Gentleman

Introduction

One of the mottos of the Dominican Order is "to contemplate and to share with others the fruits of our contemplation." Most Dominicans over the centuries have done that sharing through pulpit preaching and classroom teaching. There have always been some Dominicans, however, who took the preaching "road less travelled by." Fra Angelico, Fra Juan Mayno and Fra Bartolomeo shared the fruits of their contemplation through their paintings. Blessed James of Ulm did the same with his stained glass windows. Blessed James of Voragine organized a troupe of jugglers and acrobats to combine preaching and entertainment. Hyacinth Besson shared through his drawings while tertiary Sigrid Undset did the same through her novels. In our own time in the United States Dominicans such as Fathers Urban Nagle, Gilbert Hartke, and Peter John Cameron have exercised their preaching ministry through the theatre. Father Thomas McGlynn, Father Angelo Zarlenga and Sister Mary of the Compassion followed in the foot steps of Angelico, Mayno and Bartolomeo.

Using the art of poetry as a means of sharing the harvest of our contemplation goes back at least as far as Saint Thomas Aquinas whose poetic works, *Adoro Te, Pange Lingua, Lauda Sion* and *Verbum Supernum*, became the lyrics of hymns still sung today. Father Vincent McNabb praised Aquinas as "bard of Christ" in his poem, *Saint Thomas*. We remember Blessed Henry Suso for many things, not the least of which are his poems such as *Spring Song, What Thou Art to Me* and *The Finding*.

The good poet, like the person who preaches well in other forms, strives, for others, to give external form to the discoveries and insights of his or her interior life. The American poet Edwin Markham wrote that "the poet is a dweller between two worlds, the seen and the unseen; he beholds objects and events in their larger outline and deeper mystery... His mission is an eternal quest for the absolute reality and verity which is behind the senses." Preachers who choose poetry do so because they think that the poem is the best medium to impart their particular message. A sermon from a pulpit or a lecture in a classroom may be the better channel for communicating an idea or a body of knowledge. The poem may be the better means of expressing an image, experience, emotion or vision. As Father Benedict Ashley wrote "I find poetry, even if it descends to doggerel, can often express the analogies required by spiritual events better than abstract prose." The best poets, whether they think of themselves as religious or not, strive to find and express goodness, truth and beauty; which is to say, the Divine. Theodore Soares wrote in *Finding God Through the Beautiful,* "Religious experience, the concepts and practices of religion—shot through as they are with feelings and values—reach out naturally to poetry as its most fitting vehicle of expression"

The title of this anthology, *Oranges From Dominic's Tree,* comes from the tradition that Saint Dominic planted an orange tree in the garden of the Priory of Santa Sabina in Rome. A series of oranges trees have grown in that garden for almost nine hundred years, each taken from a shoot of the previous tree. (In her poem, *The Orange Leaf,* Sister Mary Stanislaus McCarthy commemorates that tree.) Dominic's tree still produces oranges. The orange is an appropriate metaphor for the poem. A good poem, like a good orange, should be small, beautiful, flavorful and nourishing. The reader or the listener should be drawn to its compact beauty, enjoy the experience of consuming it and, ultimately, be nourished by it. We might also compare a poem to a preached retreat, a series of lectures or a theological treatise as we might compare a delicately carved cameo to a wall size mural. One is not better than the other because of size; in its own way each can draw the listener/ reader/ viewer toward goodness, truth and beauty. Some great sermons and books survive the ages. So do some poems. A person may remember the lines of a cherished and meaningful poem for a lifetime. Father George Cochran express this well in *For Meg, Who Wanted a Poem*: "Color fades as the dead leaf curls, but a poem will sing in your brain forever."

Reading poems in the back of the breviary (the book of the Divine Office) prompted me to begin to collect spiritual poems for personal meditation and prayer. Because of my background in both speech and English I have long been interested in the oral performance of poetry and for many years I taught a course in the oral interpretation of poetry. (To experience the pleasure of spoken poetry, read Father Damian Magrath's *Creation* out loud or ask someone to read it to you.) Those factors, combined with my desire to preserve the literary works of Dominicans, culminated in the creation of this book.

This anthology celebrates the creative sharing through poetry of the fruits of the contemplation of thirty-three Dominicans. The fourteen friars, ten sisters and nine members of what was formerly known as the Third Order wrote and published in English from the early nineteenth century to the present. Several, such as Father Paul Murray, Brother Antoninus and Mother Rose Hawthorne, are well known. Others are nearly forgotten or neglected talents such as Michael Field, the pen name of two women tertiaries; and John Gray, rumored to have been the inspiration for Oscar Wilde's novel, The *Picture of Dorian Gray*. In the subtitle of this book I have used the term "selected poems" because there may well be Dominicans who have published in English that I have overlooked. This is the result of my shortcoming as a researcher and not of the quality of their poems. With that limitation in mind, I hope that the reader will come to recognize and appreciate poetry as an authentic sharing of the fruits of contemplation.

- Matthew Powell, O.P.

Contents

Introduction .... *iv*

Father Benedict M. Ashley, O.P. 1
    Dominican Serving Mass Early on an Autumn Morning 1
    Fear of Drowning 3
    Heart Transplant 4
    The Fourth Beatitude 5

Sister Elizabeth Michael Boyle, O.P. 7
    The View from fhe Ruin 7
    Easter Rebellion 8
    To All the Unknown Soldiers 9

Sister Imelda Brady, O.P. 11
    Thus Shall It Ever Be 11
    Et Incarnatus Est. 12

Sister Maryanna Childs, O.P. 13
    Meditations in a Museum Cloister 13
    To a Medieval Madonna in a Modern Décor 14
    With One Swift Thought 14
    Garmenting 15
    Sonnet for Seven Americans 16

Father George Leonard Cochran, O.P. Error! Bookmark not defined.
    For Meg, Who Wanted a Poem 18
    The Art of Dying 18
    A Refusal to Apologize 19
    Boarding House 20
    The Bicycle 20
    Village Idiot 22
    Teaching My Students to Write 23
    The Wake 24

Klutz 24
　　Physically Phit! 25
　　Points of View 25
　　Small Boys, Tall Tales 26
Eleanor Cecilia Donnelly 27
　　Misunderstandings 27
　　The Lady President's Ball 29
Sister Mary Jean Dorcy, O.P. 31
　　At the Well, Bethlehem 31
　　Doors 32
Sister Mary Alphonsus Downing, O.P. 34
　　The Prayer of Father Dominic 35
Mother Francis Raphael Drane, O.P. 37
　　What the Soul Desires 37
　　Disappointment 39
Father Edwin Essex, O.P. 41
　　Loneliness 41
　　Cor Ad Cor 42
　　The Good Thief 42
　　The Brother 43
　　Epigram 43
Brother Antoninus Everson, O.P. 44
　　Out of the Ash 44
　　The Encounter 45
Michael Field 47
　　A Summer Wind 47
　　Descent from the Cross 48
　　Fellowship 50
　　Marionettes 51
　　Qui Renovat Juventutem Meam 51

Introduction

Aridity 52
Sister Mary Jeremy Finnegan, O.P. **53**
    The Candle Lighter 53
    Homage 54
Ruth Mary Fox **56**
    Of Words 56
    When I At Last Am Come To Die 57
    Prayer For The First Day Of School 58
    Some Did Return 58
Father Francis Augustine Gaffney, O.P. **60**
    Our Lady of the Rosary 61
    St. Patrick 61
    A Soggarth's Prayer 62
Father Henry Michael Gaffney, O.P. **63**
    Our Lady Dreams 63
    In the House of Them That Love Thee 64
John Gray **65**
    A Crucifix 66
    A Une Madone. Imitated from the French of Charles Baudelaire 67
Father Thomas Heath, O.P. **70**
    All Saints All Souls 70
    Pray for Me When I Am Dead 71
    You That Have No Lines 72
Father Armando P. Ibáñez, O.P. **73**
    Gentleness 73
    Grace 74
    Ave Maria 74
    Monastery of the Angels 75
Mother Rose Hawthorne Lathrop, O.P. **77**

Beyond Utterance..78
  The Suicide..78
  A Song Before Grief..79
  Pride: Fate..79
  Francie..80
  The Outgoing Race...81

Shane Leslie 83
  Ireland, Mother of Priests..83
  Fleet Street...85
  Mi Careme in Connaught..85
  Nightmare..86

Sister Mary Benvenuta Little, O.P. 87
  Hawkesyard...87
  Easter Thought 88
  Domini Canes 89

Father Damian Magrath, O.P. 90
  Creation 90
  Lux de Caelo Natus Est Nobis..92
  Made Flesh 92
  The Washing Of The Feet..94

Theodore Maynard 97
  At Woodchester 98
  Judas 99
  In Domo Johannis...100
  After Communion..101
  Viaticum 101
  Meekness...102
  Tragedy..103
  Ballade of a Ferocious Catholic 104

Sister Mary Stanislaus McCarthy, O.P. 106
    An Orange Leaf 106
    Napoleon's Happiest Day. 107

Father Vincent McNabb, O.P. 108
    Unto the Olive Hill 109
    Saint Thomas 109
    A Golden Jubilee. 110
    Dark Speech upon the Harp 112

Father Paul Murray, O.P. 113
    Second Youngest 113
    The First Wisdom 115
    Threshold 116
    In the Making 116

Hilary Pepler 118
    The Law The Lawyers Know About 118

Father Peter Pius Portier, O.P. 119
    To Modesty 119

Father Christopher Renz, O.P. 121
    Lauds 121
    Lauds 122
    Soil in Autumn 123

Father Dominic Rover, O.P. 124
    ARS MORIENDI: The Art Of Dying 124
    The Sunflower 130

Emily Steward Shapcote 131
    Mary, The Perfect Woman 131

Acknowledgements 133

Credits 134

Compiler and Editor 135

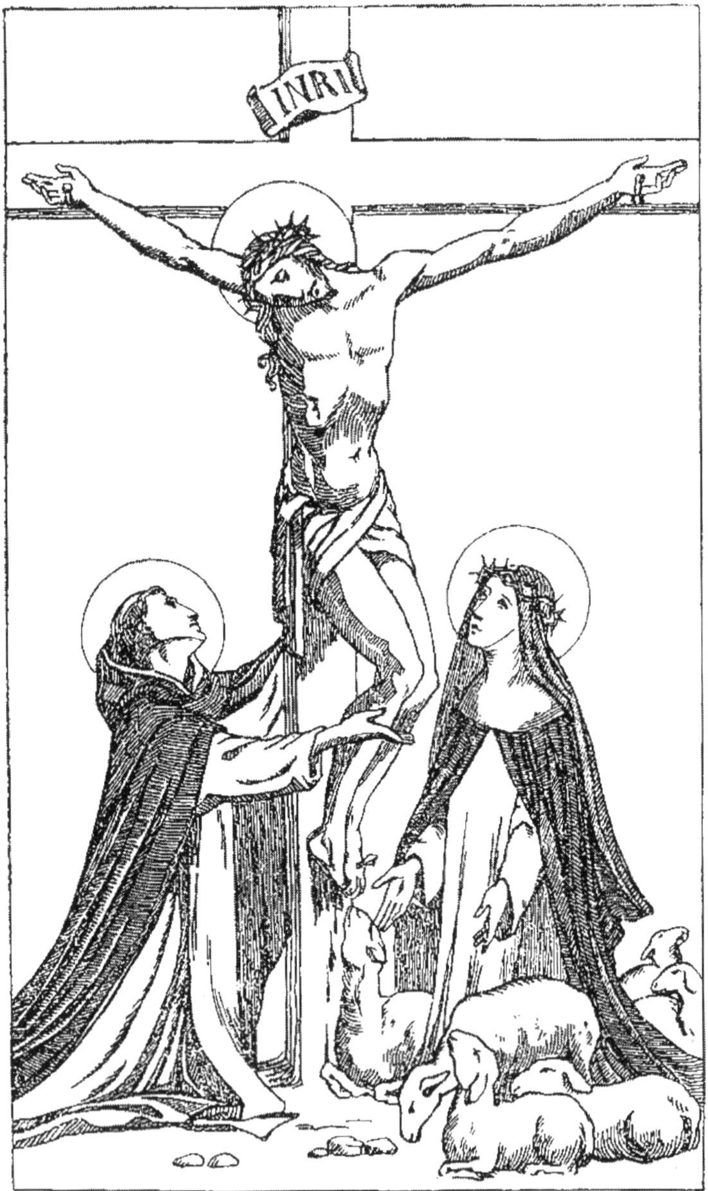

R.P. BESSON PINXT L. ROISIN DEL

Father Benedict M. Ashley, O.P.

Winston Ashley was born in Blackwell, Oklahoma in 1915 and began writing poetry as a boy. Hoping to be a writer, he received a scholarship to the University of Chicago where he earned a master's degree in comparative literature. While at Chicago Ashley won the John Billings Fiske Prize for Poetry and published his first poems in *Poetry* magazine. As a young man he was a committed communist and atheist. Studying the works of Saint Thomas Aquinas under Mortimer Adler, however, he converted to Catholicism in 1938. He then earned a doctorate in political science at the University of Notre Dame. In 1942 Ashley entered the Dominican Order where he received the name Benedict Mary. After ordination in 1948, Father Ashley earned a Ph.D. in philosophy and became a major exponent of what became known as the "River Forest School" of Thomism. He taught at numerous institutions including Aquinas Institute of Philosophy and Theology, Saint Louis University and the Pontifical John Paul II Institute. During his long career he wrote nineteen books, including *Health Medical Ethics*, which continues to be a fundamental text in Catholic medical ethics. Despite his busy life, Father Ashley never lost his love of poetry. He continued to research and write until shortly before his death at the age of ninety-seven.

Dominican Serving Mass Early on an Autumn Morning

The green vestments wrinkling with gold
and the smooth white linen,
the window glazed with redeeming sunrise,
the purple night rejected
by gray light,
the strong points of the candles not yet blunted

by gray light—

Here the senses as they awaken prickle with color,
the smell of wax, of wine, wool,
beads rattled against a silent wall, water dripping,
the ache of sleep, the stillness and the damp-
under my black cloak should be white prayer.

The senses awaking irritated
are as this realm of broken color in the realm of the Greater Silence,
within dark corridors, rays of sensation in the dull body.
Yet now at the center of the smoothed linen
white bread, deep wine
lie ready.

So in the soul the blank mind is bright and stamped
with the Name and with the Cross.
The will's the chalice in which self-love's three drops
are lost in Love
and these await the Word,
fruit of long sun and labor, rain and the enriched wind.
My mind furnishes no thought.
Imagination fretted like sleepy eyes;
its ear tormented by the bell,
the Latin drone presents no blessed Face.
taste thickened, seeks not even sweetness,
and all appetite looks back to the dark and to death.
Yet mind retains the habitual seal,
the will its graven hollow.

Sleepless God-Manity be Thou by my unthought Thought
within these emptied species of my mind,

the unmoved Love
within the surface of this sparkless wine.

Fear of Drowning

Silence and the waves of chanting
of psalms that rage, plead, praise,
through seasonal fasts and feasts,
the days, the nights, sun or moon
filling the silence before the Mystery veiled
in the gilded tabernacle,
fear overwhelming me
that I had let go. Your hand
stretched out to me like to Peter
sensing his feet were sinking,
panic, terror, plunging
into the chaos of doubt, despair,
drowning, gasping for air.

Yet you were there.
In the dark I could see
the spark of the tabernacle-lamp on its stand,
as though the dark there was your hand reaching out.
Like Thomas I felt the healing wound in your hand
that would heal
my doubt.
Under my feet in the receding waves
I felt
firm the Living Rock.

HEART TRANSPLANT

Father Ashley wrote this poem after observing Dr. Michael DeBakey perform open heart surgery at Methodist Hospital in Houston.

Crushed in the sick mob of the poor
I stretch my contagious hands to touch you, Jesus alive!
Against your healing hands my breath is foul.
Bend, breathe life
again into my slime!

In a white room
green doctors excise a pale, bruised heart,
sew in a dead man's red, hot heart,
shock it to beat and to keep its beat
until the dying body of the still living, too far gone
rejects . . .

Doomed life retains the strength to kill.

In a ghetto
Before a dying church
A statue of the Sacred Heart spreads wide its arms
Its lifeless marble leached by slimy rain.
The temple's granite walls crumble to let
In creeping, crawling things.

O Heart, you come again
to cut open our bodies, to thrust in your hand,
to tear out this dead lump, to drop back in the mud,
to stitch into the shocked body your healing life,
your Heart, You
Live in dying Me.

Too far gone?
Will my corruption, gasping to live,
reject?

THE FOURTH BEATITUDE

Blessed be the hungry!
    Through the labyrinthine supermart
    I push my loaded cart,
    down aisles, aisles, aisles
    of glorious packages,
    cans, bottles, jars,
    cellophane wrapped meats
    and even greeting cards
    whispering love for birthdays,
    cuddly bunnies for Easter,
    violet condolences for the dead
    whose mouths, closed finally
    hunger no more.

Not by bread alone
    nor all my supermarket's plenty
    am I ever filled
    with honest joy,
    if still my heart is empty
    as a glass of soured wine
    poured in the thirsting dust.

Yet blessed will my hunger be,
    if that hunger, if that thirst
    will be to share my bread, give drink;

       to fill my empty heart
       with all the fullness
       the overflowing plenty
       of the poor now fed
       of the thirsty
       taking at least a sip
       of joy.

Not by bread alone or rather
       not by cellophane wrapped bread,
       sliced thin for those who have to diet
       after consuming the portions of the poor;
       but by the bread of honest work,
       honest words,
       common life
       summed up
       in Jesus' body, Jesus' blood,
       for the blessing of those who hunger and who thirst
       for justice, and in forgiveness make peace

.

Sister Elizabeth Michael Boyle, O.P.

Sister Elizabeth Michael Boyle, a member of the Dominican Sisters of Caldwell, New Jersey, is professor emeritus of English at Caldwell College. She earned an M.A. from the Catholic University of America and a Ph.D. from Drew University. A reader of poetry all of her life, Sister turned to writing poems only in her later years. In addition to her poetry, she wrote *Preaching the Poetry of the Gospels: A Lyric Companion to the Lectionary* and *Science and Metaphor: An Evolving Revelation*. Sister Elizabeth Michael received the Fra Angelico Award in 2010 for her poetry and has been inducted into the American Academy of Poets. The following poems are from her collection, *A View From The Ruin* (2011).

THE VIEW FROM FHE RUIN

It is not the ruin
but the view from the ruin
that is worth the long climb
and the risk of a fall.

It is not the temple
but the myth that built the temple
that survives
earthquakes, erosion, murder, betrayal
and the lightning bolt in the heart.

Day after day in the August sun
we ascend and descend
and ascend again
chilled to the bone in our separate solitudes:
ruins wandering the ruins
islands adrift among islands

stones communing with stones.

But it is not the ruin
but the view from the ruin
that will have been worth both climb and fall
when, back to back at the summit,
we pluck the last flower piercing the rubble
and disappear into the view.

EASTER REBELLION

At the height of the Easter season
all the women in New York
are wearing black.
What are they mourning?

The dead, the living,
the faithless departed:
spouses, offspring, fondest illusions?
or has some tsar decreed
mandatory chromophobia?

"This year color may be worn only by
children
retirees
mid-western tourists and
nuns who have exchanged
a vow to be obedient for
a vow to be unfashionable."

Standing single-file waiting for the ferry
New York's best-dressed women
look as uniform as
parochial school girls
whose catechism has expunged
spring's vulgar revelation.

"Our gaudy, wild, unruly God prefers
wardrobes of azalea and forsythia.

Heed her"

To All the Unknown Soldiers

Forgive us for what we ask you to do:
to kill
without shame
without seeing or hating those
whose names you will never know
whose children will always hate you
without ever knowing your name.

Forgive us for what we ask you to do:
to survive
by keeping your target faceless
by silencing the inner voice that knows
the one you kill is always
innocent
often someone's once-in-a-lifetime
poem, painting, song,
always someone's father, husband, son
someone's mother, wife, daughter

always your brother or sister
condemned to die
as a human shield
for inhumanity.

Forgive us, O merciful God,
for what we ask you to bless
for You, like us,
are also collateral damage.
You, like us, are another
unanticipated casualty
another prisoner of war
hopelessly missing in action
helpless to prevent
the war crimes
committed in our name.

Sister Imelda Brady, O.P.

Helen Brady, born in Jackson, Tennessee in 1868, entered the Dominican novitiate at Saint Agnes Academy in Memphis in 1887 and received the name Imelda. The Saint Agnes community was, at the time, in the process of affiliating with the Saint Catharine, Kentucky community so she was professed at Saint Catharine's. Sister Imelda later returned to teach English at Saint Agnes. Her collection of poems was published as *The Harp of Dawn and Other Poems* in 1924 and received favorable reviews from *America*, *Catholic World* and the *Boston Pilot*. Sister Imelda died in 1943 at Saint Catharine's.

Thus Shall It Ever Be

O Calumny, thy victims down the years
    Are drifting! and from weary, aching hearts
Flow ever and forever silent tears.
    The cruelty of thy envenomed darts
Doth pierce the souls of men; thine artful lies
    Besmirch the stainless names of those
Who truth and honor, love and wrong, despise,
    And all its crafty ways and wiles oppose.

I know not why, and yet I know 'tis true,
    That Wrong oppresseth Right.
    Here 'neath blue skies,
Where men in peace were wont to live and love,
    The weak are trampled by the strong, and cries
    That soar beyond the gleaming stars above,
Before the throne of God for pity sue.

ET INCARNATUS EST.

A hospice, seeketh He Who is,
    All free from sin's duress –
Each chamber lit with Purity,
    And Peace, and Holiness.

A hallowed nook where Mercy's breath,
    Like redolent perfume –
In silver censer lightly swung –
    Pervadeth each rich room.

He findeth mansion wondrous rare –
    A gleaming "House of Gold" –
And entering the oped door,
    Doth Deity unfold.

Sister Maryanna Childs, O.P.

Sister Maryanna Childs, a member of the Dominican Sisters of Saint Mary of the Springs (Columbus, Ohio) for 73 years, was born Clara Henrietta Childs in New York City in 1910. She professed her vows in 1930 and, after earning a master's degree in literary criticism from the Catholic University of America, she taught English at the College of Saint Mary of the Springs (later Ohio Dominican University) for 40 years. Sister's poems appeared in *America, Catholic World, Sign* and other Catholic magazines. In addition to poetry, Sister Maryanna wrote short stories, children's books and magazine articles. Her book, *With Love and Laughter: Reflections of a Dominican Nun*, published in 1960, is a collection of joyful memories and anecdotes of religious life. *Love Songs*, published in 1980, is a collection of her poems. In 1986 Sister won the grand prize in the Golden Poetry Contest conducted by the World of Poetry for *Sonnet for Seven Americans*, her tribute to the six astronauts and one teacher who died in the Challenger space shuttle disaster. After her death in 2003 Ohio Dominican University established the *Childs Writing Award* given annually to the outstanding student writer.

MEDITATIONS IN A MUSEUM CLOISTER

Mournful Madonnas with pathetic smiles
Hold out carved Babes to visitors with such
A wistful eagerness, a naive hope.
The printed placard says   PLEASE DO NOT TOUCH.

Consummate skill, the guide remarks.   It would behoove
The sightseer to note the item well.   The Louvre.
Contains the head.   Where are the limbs?   He does not know.
But here's the torso nailed tight to the cross. Still graceful though.

The drapery has such finesse.   The folds still keep
Their color.   Tourists nod.   Beneath John and the Virgin weep.

To a Medieval Madonna in a Modern Décor

Though not with plume or quill
These lines are written, still,
Madonna, words are said
In ball-point, liquid lead,
Or tapped out by degrees
On Olivetti's keys
That glorify your name
And magnify your fame
As when your monks of old
On vellum in clear gold,
Crimson and cobalt blue
Spelled out their love for you.

With One Swift Thought

Between us lie
The mountains and the plain,
White walls of snow, curtains of silver rain.

In this our life
Though never more we meet:
The rind is bitter but the fruit is sweet.

Prayer is a bridge
That spans the earth, the sea,
And flings its arches to eternity.

With one swift thought,
I reach God's listening heart
And there find yours, though we are leagues apart.

GARMENTING

> *Put ye on the Lord Jesus Christ.*
> *Romans xiii, 14*

Anne was the spinner
Anne spun the thread
petal soft, rosewhite,
 filament starbright
to which an angel said

    Hail, full of grace!

Mary was the weaver
weaving on the loom
fair-flesh of Christ
fabric unpriced
in her virginal womb

    God's dwelling place.

Christ is the cloth
 stretched upon a tree
temple-veil nail-rent
silken sheath blood-sprent
sheer humanity

    cloaking God's face!

Anne was the spinner
Mary was the thread
Christ is the cloth
We are garmented.

SONNET FOR SEVEN AMERICANS

The whole world watched the silver shuttle rising
Into the morning light and breathed a prayer
As that bright wonderment of man's devising
Engraved a shining arc upon the air.

But seconds later, smoke puffs and a flaming
Fire-tongue blossomed to a hideous rose!
Fear gripped the watching world beyond all naming;
In disbelief the friends and loved ones froze.

This is a little song for those brave seven:
Six astronauts, a teacher who loved space.
They soared into the sky and there found heaven;
Cast off earth's bounds, reached up and touched God's face.

As strong and joyous then, despite our tears,
We shall remember them though all our years.

Father George Leonard Cochran, O.P.

George Cochran was born in Tampa, Florida in 1928 and lived through the tough economic times of the Great Depression. He spent his youth in several cities in the southern United States. He worked in advertising and journalism before joining the Air Force, serving in Germany. In 1955 he entered the Dominican novitiate at Saint Peter Martyr Priory in Winona, Minnesota. He received the religious name of Leonard, a name under which he published his poetry. In 1962 Father Cochran was ordained a priest at Saint Rose Priory in Dubuque, Iowa. A year later he was assigned to Fenwick High School in Oak Park, Illinois where he taught English for sixteen years. Father Cochran earned an M.A. and Ph.D. in English from Loyola University of Chicago; his research centered on the poems of Gerard Manley Hopkins, about whom he became a recognized authority. In 1980 he joined the faculty of Providence College in Rhode Island to teach English and philosophy. In 2008, due to declining health, he went to live under the care of the Dominican Sisters at Saint Mary of the Springs in Columbus, Ohio. Father Cochran died there in 2013.

Father Cochran published more than a hundred poems and hymn lyrics in over a half century of writing. His works appeared *in Atlantic Monthly, Harvard Magazine, Yankee Magazine, Poetry, America, Commonweal, Spirit* and other journals. In 1971 some of his poems were included in the Diamond Anniversary Anthology of Poems of the Poetry Society of America. In 1998 Father Cochran won *Yankee Magazine's* Annual Award for Best Poem and in 1999 he was awarded the Foley Poetry Prize from *America* magazine. In 2001 Providence College bestowed on him the President's Distinguished Faculty Award.

For Meg, Who Wanted a Poem

Asking for a poem is not
The same as asking for the time,
Or a light, or some slight
Thing. In the measured rhyme

Of the poem a heart beats.
Time is come and gone,
The match flares bits
Of light, then dies on

Breath whose own brief life
Affects no other thing.
Color fades as the dead leaf
Curls, but a poem will sing

In your brain forever.

The Art of Dying

    For L.M.C.

L.M.C. was Father Cochran's mother.

You took a month of days to take your leave,
going in sprints, each breath an apology,
while Spring shouted through the low window,
arguing attention from one who had no mind
for staying longer the steps of her departure.

There had been that day you fell in the street
(to which we, with the certitude of the ignorant,
attributed your illness), but went to work none-
theless, because someone there depended on you.
Another time, you made me keep a bargain made.

I shall remember you, tiny in your big bed,
who thought your need our inconvenience.
You taught me the best and simplest skills,
a right way to do all things, even this.

A REFUSAL TO APOLOGIZE

The bitterest tears are those that will not come
Despite the steady proddings of remorse.
 A heart denied release must seek some
Other clear and less resistant course

To follow; perhaps, a boisterous kind of speech
(Always a handy antidote to thought);
Again, a turning inward, beyond the reach
Of reason's sweet accord; or guilt that's bought

And paid for. Then, because I could not cry,
You said I lacked the poetry of pain
(Whetever that may mean). Even so, I
Still can't make my way against the grain:

You won't forgive the slight, however slight,
I won't unsay the world that caused the fight.

BOARDING HOUSE

During the depression, young George Cochran and his parents were forced by economic circumstances to live in a boarding house. It remained a sad memory for him.

For a young boy, there were some
rewards: the turret room at the edge
of the big house, where he could come
to play steamboat, leaning on the edge
to take imaginary soundings, mark
the concrete river's depth. Or,
times at table when grownup talk
would turn to the might-be-war
in Hitler's Europe. (Then, he thought
such a thing adventurous, being nine
and reading overmuch. He fought
toy soldiers across the dining room table
when its owner's wife
was out shopping). But some thread
ran untrue in the child's life,
altered its pattern in a manner he had
no way of grasping, a missing part
whose palpable, unidentified gloom
shadowed each day's start
Nobody's home in nobody's home.

THE BICYCLE

He never had one, money lacking.
Riding was a sign of maturity,

A passage rite. So, taking
Fear as well as temerity

Into his hands, asked the Cub
Scout master to teach a skill.
Then, on the day, fearing to flub
The whole thing and so fill

Out the requirements for failure,
Rose early, thinking activity
Might assist him to secure
Some measure of certainty.

He puttered more than usual,
Wiped dishes, offered chores done
(More than usual). The cool
Hand of his mother tested for run-

ning a fever, but all was well.
(The problem was in his knees.)
Now, it is time; nor does he tell
Anyone. His mind's eye sees

Success or failure as private,
Something to announce at choice.
For now, must not be a little late,
Must gather the manly voice

For the manly greeting, casual clasp
Of the hand, diffident smile.
No nerves, now, firm grasp
Of the handlebars. The Last Mile.

(He then knows how the condemned feel.)
Then, up, leg over, astride
At last. "Go!" Pushes the wheel.
No choice but fall or ride.

And he rides. Oh! how he rides!
He breathes deep achievement,
Racing heart outruns the strides
Of his friends' merriment.

Mastery is man's best end,
Its reach his last full laugh,
Time well spent to bend
Straight the too twisted self.

VILLAGE IDIOT

The girls were not so bad,
But we boys would call him mad,
Tag after, mock
His silent back.
Then he, not knowing,
Clapped hands, joining
The merriment,
While we rolled
Grassward, uncontrolled
In our mean humor.

It was all clean fun,
We thought, because the one
Thus chided

Was so decided
By nature thick
In wits, not quick
As we. But once
I saw straight
Into his eyes,
And there was pity
There, and surprise.

Teaching My Students to Write

Winner of the Foley Prize presented by America magazine.

I tell them it's as easy as walking:
Just put one word in front of another
Until you reach the end of the line.
Amused by the image, they grant me
A moment's attention before minds
Unmoored begin to drift. I ask them
To write about their hopes for the future,
Then watch as heads bend above
The arctic emptiness of new notebooks.
At first one or two, then a few more
Look up, into space, gathering from some
Distant country the words they will use
To tell me how perfect their lives will be
Until they reach the end of the line.

THE WAKE

Stubborn, I refused to view
the body, afraid to trace,
for memory's sake, a face
unlike the one I knew,

but kept in mind a day,
and her, so frail before
the partly open door,
calling me in from play.

KLUTZ

The perfectly thrown pass had always been just that,
Too perfect to fall into his schoolboy embrace.
Nor would he ever forget the look on the old man's face
That day the new car, its brake so casually set,
Went, as in a slow motion film, down the leaning street
Through patches of park to a sun-specked lake.
Once, he had even tried learning to tie the lures
His grandfather waved at acrobatic trout,
Until, baffled by supple thread, gave it up,
Salvaging, instead, a few more details of failure.
Today, he sits in a swatch of light, a hunched scholar
Bending among books to pick the perfect word.

Physically Phit!

He jogged by day,
by glooms of night;
breathed deeply,
considered it right
to stay in shape;
pondered knowingly
the fate of friends
whose frank obesity
weighed more on him
than on them. Caught
up in such reveries,
he plied thoughts
of a *mens sana,* etc.
transcending by far
the mundane reality
of an oncoming car.

Points of View

Who hasn't jumped
to a conclusion
now and then?
Still, it's a dance

that often leads
to confusion:

how tell a friend
(garden praising)

who spots aphids
on my plants

that bugs are what
I'm raising?

SMALL BOYS, TALL TALES

Our ancient neighbor rode his rocking-chair
Out of the past and into our lives,
Feeding us tales of how he'd talked his way
Out of trouble, convincing the cannibals,
At the last moment, not to light the fire;
More wonderful yet, how he'd made do
With bare hands when the twin-barreled rifle,
For no apparent reason, failed to fire.

Of course, the turncoat facts betrayed him.
Trails he'd never tracked called him liar
Even as he mapped out new adventures.
Not that it mattered to us, who longed to live
In a world where truth was a movable feast.

Eleanor Cecilia Donnelly

Eleanor Cecilia Donnelly, born in Philadelphia in 1838, was a poet, short story writer and biographer. She began writing as a child and her family encouraged her literary talents and often hosted prominent Catholic writers and intellectuals. As a girl she considered being a nun, but in early adulthood she joined the Third Order of Saint Dominic. A prolific writer, during her lifetime she published over thirty books and hundreds of poems including verses for children. Her poetry largely addresses Catholic and spiritual themes, although she did write a series of Civil War poems in the declamatory style common in the nineteenth century. When Donnelly died in 1917 the Philadelphia *Catholic Standard and Times* described her as "one of the foremost Catholic women poets of America."

MISUNDERSTANDINGS

How like unsightly worms they ceaseless crawl
Under the pleasant roses of our lives,
Gnawing and gnawing, till the fresh leaves fall,
And nothing green or beautiful survives.

Leaving a ruin of corroding slime
That which was fair and wholesome just before;
Ah, tell us not new buds will grow in time!
These precious plants will never blossom more.

Now 'tis a false report; anon, a glance
Sidelong, but with no secret malice fraught:
We press our hearts, as though a poisoned lance
Had pierced them, and a bleeding fissure wrought.

Then 'tis a chain of trifles (as we think)
Lighter than feathers blown into the air, --
But when rude hands have forged them link by link,
We clank our iron fetters in despair.

And straightway, 'twixt our own and some dear heart,
A nameless, viewless barrier is set;
And lives, long mingled, flow, thenceforth, part
Unto one common ocean of regret.

And though we strove to carve, as sculptors do,
Our stony trials into shapes serene,
Our noblest image of the pure and true
Would be, just then, denounced as base and mean.

Ah, it is hard to hold our souls in peace,
To keep our spirits sunny, while these things
Haunt us, like evil birds, and never cease
Making the sunshine dusty with their wings!

But there is One who understands it all:
The wounded heart that 'neath the olive trees,
And on the Mount, in bitterness let fall
The secret of its own vast agonies.

And we may trust our faults and failures, too,
Unto His love, as humble children should;
Content that if all others misconstrue,
By Him, at least, our hearts are understood.

The Lady President's Ball

In this poem, from her Civil War series, Donnelly contrasts a ball given by the First Lady, Mary Todd Lincoln, at the White House with the plight of a dying soldier in a military hospital nearby.

"The lights in the President's mansion,
The gas-lights are cheery and red,
I see them glowing and glancing,
As I toss on my wearisome bed.
I see them gemming the windows,
And, starlike, studding the hall,
Where the tide of fashion flows inward
To the Lady President's Ball.

"My temples are throbbing with fever,
My limbs are palsied with pain;
And the crash of the festal music
Burns into my aching brain, —
Till I rave with delirious fancies
And coffin and bier and pall
Mix up with the flower and laces
Of my Lady President's Ball.

"What matter that I, poor private,
Lie here on my narrow bed,
With the fever scorching my vitals
And dazing my hapless head?
What matters that nurses are callous,
And rations are meager and small,
So long as the beau monde revel
At the Lady President's Ball?

"Who pities my poor old mother,
Who comforts my sweet young wife,
Alone in the distant city,
With sorrow sapping their life?
I have no money to send them;
They cannot come to my call.
No money? Yet hundreds are wasting
At my Lady President's Ball!

"Hundreds, ay, hundreds of thousands
In satins, jewels and wine;
French dishes for dainty stomachs,
(While the black broth sickens mine!)
And jellies and fruits and cool ices,
And fountains that flash as they fall:
Oh, God! For a cup of cold water
From the Lady President's Ball!

"Nurse! Bring me my uniform ragged,
Ah! Why did you blow out the light?
Help me up. though I'm aching and giddy,
I must go to my dear ones tonight.
Wife! Mother! grown weary with waiting —
I'm coming, I'll comfort ye all…"

And the private sank dead while they reveled
At my Lady President's Ball.

Sister Mary Jean Dorcy, O.P.

Frances Emma Dorcy was born in Anacortes, Washington in 1914. After her freshman year at the University of Washington, she entered the Dominican Sisters of Everett, Washington where she received the name Sister Mary Jean. After receiving her bachelor's degree from Gonzaga University she earned a master of fine arts degree from the California College of Art and Craft. Sister Mary Jean is best known for her black and white paper cut silhouettes which illustrated many books. Also an avid writer, she produced biographies of saints, poems and books for children and teenagers. Sister's poems about Mary were published as *Our Lady of Springtime*. All Dominicans are familiar with her book, *Saint Dominic's Family,* the lives and legends of 339 Dominicans published by Priory Press in 1964 and translated into Spanish, German and Chinese. Sister Mary Jean died in 1988 and is buried at the convent cemetery in Everett.

AT THE WELL, BETHLEHEM

So very quietly she came
We really did not get her name.
The man was clever with his hands
And quick in serving my demands –
He more than paid the fair amount
(That cave's of very small account).

They only stayed a little while
It's strange the way I miss her smile.
The very poorest stuff, her cloak
Yet she behaved like kingly folk;
Although it seems unlikely such
Would come, for Bethlehem's not much.

(Some dusty story; people say
A prophet mentioned it one day.)

The Baby? Yes, a lovely Son –
He wrung my heart, that little One;
Reminded me, somehow, of all
 My mother meant when I was small
Of how she'd read me with her eyes –
A person doesn't realize.

The census? Yes, we did quite well;
Inns filled before the darkness fell.
Aside from that, a tiresome year.
Nothing ever happens here.

Doors

Wide is the path to Caesar's house,
And marble paves the floor,
But rough and narrow the lonely way
That leads to a stable door.
And none but the small ones may enter in,
For the door is low and small
Where He sleeps on the world's one stainless throne
Who is Ruler and Lord of all.

Caesar is counting his hosts today,
Recording the gainful hands,
For feet that walk on a marble way
Are fettered with iron bands;

And only the shepherds are poor enough
To gaze at a midnight sky
And kneel in awe where the Queen of Heaven
Is singing a lullaby.

They are splendid roads that are Caesar's roads.
And great is the power of Rome;
But a star is bright in a darkened sky.
Higher than Roman eagles fly
And further than exiles roam.

O wanderer, come where the small ones are,
To the gate that is lighted with light of star,
Where the heaven's King and His Mother are,
The gate that leads all men home.

Sister Mary Alphonsus Downing, O.P.

Mary Ellen Downing, who became known as Sister Mary Alphonsus, was born in Cork, Ireland in 1828. While in her teens she became active in the movement for Irish independence and wrote for the nationalist newspaper, *The United Irishmen*. Downing once wrote to a friend, "If I get a tooth ache it will be through means of the English, clenching my teeth when I think of them and look at the country they have darkened!" In 1848 the British government cracked down on the movement and arrested most of her friends. It brought an end to the group. In 1849 Downing entered the Presentation Sisters, but ill health forced her to leave after one year. Shortly thereafter she joined the Third Order of Saint Dominic with Mother Mary Imelda, prioress general of the Dominican Sisters of Drogheda, as her spiritual director. Though a tertiary she became known to everyone by her profession name. As Sister Mary Alphonsus she wrote over 500 poems, but few rise above pious verse. After her death in 1869, friends collected her poems into a book, *Voices from the Heart*.

The Prayer of Father Dominic

SAITH Saint Dominic to his chosen,
"If the seed be put to keep,
It will moulder to corruption,
And no fruit shall any reap."

Saith, Saint Dominic to his chosen,
"If the seed be cast abroad,
It will bring forth in due season
For the reaping hand of God."
Then, in wonder at his boldness,
But all trusting to his word,
His little flock divided
For the mission of the Lord;

And it calmed the grief of parting
From their Master and their home,
To think upon their Saviour,
And the harvest time to come.

But one bent down all trembling
And, beseeching not to go,
Said, his thought was ever feeble,
And his speech was ever slow;

He looked to no conversion
And he dreamed of no reward,
He feared but to dishonour
The high mission of the Lord:

Then Saint Dominic, kindly soothing,
Laid a blessing on his head,
And, "twice before the Altar
I will think of thee," he said;

"At the sunrise and the sunset,
Still a father's prayer shall he
That the God for whom thou strivest
May be armour unto thee."

Then the young man rose up strengthened
And went forth upon his way
And, he never failed in preaching
Who dared simply to obey;

But the fervor of his feeling
And the grandeur of his word
Still gave proof that Father Dominic
Was in prayer before the Lord

Mother Francis Raphael Drane, O.P.

Born in London, England in 1823 to an Anglican family, Augusta Theodosia Drane converted to Catholicism in 1850 and entered the Dominican Sisters of Stone. She received the religious name, Sister Francis Raphael. Since Drane was already a published author when she entered the community, however, she continued to write under her former name. She served as mistress of novices and then mistress of studies. Elected prioress general in 1881, she continued in office until her death in 1894. Mother Francis Raphael produced nineteen books of catechetics, history, biography, drama and poetry. Among her works are a two volume definitive biography of Saint Catherine of Siena and a biography of Saint Dominic. Her poems were collected in *Songs in the Night*.

WHAT THE SOUL DESIRES

> *There Thou wilt show me what my soul desired;*
> *There Thou wilt give at once, O my Life, what Thou gavest me the other day!"*
> *(Spiritual Canticle, Stanza xxxviii)*

In this poem the author expresses her frustration about a fleeting mystical experience that never occurred again. The poem was reprinted in "The Oxford Book of Mystical Verse."

There is a rapture that my soul desires,
There is a something that I cannot name;
I know not after what my soul aspires,
Nor guess from whence the restless longing came;
But ever from my childhood have I felt it,
In all things beautiful and all things gay,

And ever has its gentle, unseen presence
Fallen, like a shadow-cloud, across my way.

It is the melody of all sweet music,
In all fair forms it is the hidden grace;
In all I love, a something that escapes me,
Flies my pursuit, and ever veils its face.
I see it in the woodland's summer beauty,
I hear it in the breathing of the air;
I stretch my hands to feel for it, and grasp it,
But ah! too well I know, it is not there.

In sunset-hours, when all the earth is golden,
And rosy clouds are hastening to the west,
I catch a waving gleam, and then 'tis vanished,
And the old longing once more fills my breast.
It is not pain, although the fire consumes me,
Bound up with memories of my happiest years;
It steals into my deepest joys - O mystery!
It mingles, too, with all my saddest tears.

Once, only once, there rose the heavy curtain,
The clouds rolled back, and for too brief a space
I drank in joy as from a living fountain,
And seemed to gaze upon it, face to face:
But of that day and hour who shall venture
With lips untouched by seraph's fire to tell?
I saw Thee, O my Life! I heard, I touched Thee, -
Then o'er my soul once more the darkness fell.

The darkness fell, and all the glory vanished;
I strove to call it back, but all in vain:
O rapture! to have seen it for a moment!

O anguish! that it never came again!
That lightening-flash of joy that seemed eternal,
Was it indeed but wandering fancy's dream?
Ah, surely no! that day the heavens opened,
And on my soul there fell a golden gleam.

O Thou, my Life, give me what then Thou gavest!
No angel vision do I ask to see,
I seek no ecstasy of mystic rapture,
Nought, nought, my Lord, my Life, but only Thee!
That golden gleam hath purged my sight, revealing
In the fair ray reflected from above,
Thyself, beyond all sight, beyond all feeling,
The hidden Beauty, and the hidden Love.

As the hart panteth for the water-brooks,
And seeks the shades whence cooling fountains burst;
Even so for Thee, O Lord, my spirit fainteth,
Thyself alone hath power to quench its thirst.
Give me what then Thou gavest, for I seek it
No longer in Thy creatures, as of old;
I strive no more to grasp the empty shadow,
The secret of my life is found and told!

DISAPPOINTMENT
An Epitaph

O STRANGER! wouldst thou know
Whose dust unhonoured moulders here below?
His was no scutcheon of emblazoned pride,
Ask not his name, enough he lived and died.

His life was vanity:
Swift as the rippling tide it floated by;
Its beauty was the beauty of a dream,
He gathered flowers to cast them in the stream.

He won no victor's crown,
In Life's fierce combat early smitten down,
The tramp of hurrying crowds swept o'er his head,
And left him lying there among the dead.

How could he win the prize?
Men counted him as feeble and unwise;
They said he failed in all he had to do,
He bowed his head, and meekly owned it true.

He knew it must be so:
Some hearts for chorus-tones are pitched too low;
The strings of his had borne too tight a strain,
At the first chord he struck they snapped in twain.

Dost thou despise him, friend?
Know that each soul is born for its own end;
Nor is success the standard, for in heaven
A double bliss to broken hearts is given.

Defeated, yet resigned,
The patient heart that lacked the master-mind,
To such as him, what gift had earth to give?
He lived to suffer, and he died to live.

Father Edwin Essex, O.P.

Born in England in 1891, Edwin Essex entered the Dominican novitiate in 1909. After ordination he served in a variety of ministries, including being a naval chaplain and editor of the journal, *Blackfriars*. His book, *From a Chaplain's Log*, chronicles his naval experience. Father Essex also established the priory at Edinburgh, Scotland in 1932. He spent his later years in South Africa where he was, for a time, vicar provincial. In addition to poetry, Father Essex wrote twenty four short stories for *Irish Rosary Magazine*. His books include two collections of poetry, *Poems* (1923) and *Song of Wisdom and Other Poems* (1933). He died in 1966. These poems are from his 1923 collection.

LONELINESS

MY soul has solitudes
    Where no pace falls;
Thy silent trespassings
    No man forestalls.

My soul has silences
    No voice can break;
Only Thy hidden words
    Its echoes wake.

But, O, the solitudes
    Shouldst Thou not come!
The stricken silences
    When Thou art dumb!

Cor Ad Cor

I HAVE praised Thee in the words of other men,
And cried to Thee with other men's lament,
Yea, sung with their beauty, sorrowed with their tears,
But, O, my soul is not content, content.

I am tired of yielding Thee but borrowed thoughts,
Weary of bringing Thee the daily loan
I must get from men and books and strangers' eyes -
Now would I find one prayer that is my own!

The Good Thief

THIEF, over-bold,
In one last exploit failed, condemned; untold
     Thy deeds remain
That purchased for thee this extremest pain.

     But not less thief
Art thou for this kind silence. This thy chief
     And final theft
Of Pardon brands thee robber doubly-deft!

The Brother

> *This young man . . . whose feet refused the dance and whose lips declined the beaker when the Prodigal Son came home to his prodigal father.*
>   - Rev. Vincent McNabb, O.P.

LIKE son, like father! Both would spend their all,
One his fair substance on a harlot's whim,
The other, of his goods more prodigal,
       To set the youth at large and welcome him!

But that proud brother, jealous of his right,
       Held all he had, and closed his hand and heart
Against both earth and heaven; so out of sight
       And hearing of all joy he sulks apart.

Epigram

So must outlive we even earth and sky,
Thou, God, and I, in one persistent Now.
And when Eternity is old then Thou
Shalt still be young, but how much younger I!

Brother Antoninus Everson, O.P.

William Everson, poet, printer, literary critic and, for a time, a Dominican friar, was born on a farm near Sacramento, California in 1912. Both of his parents were printers. After attending college for two years, he moved to San Francisco. Refusing to fight during World War II, he spent two years in a work camp for conscientious objectors. After release he became part of the San Francisco Poetry Renaissance. To the surprise of his literary friends, Everson converted to Catholicism in 1948. Further shocking friends, in 1951 he entered the Dominicans at Saint Albert's Priory in Oakland, taking the name Brother Antoninus. Two previous civil marriages delayed his profession of vows for several years and, until then, he lived in the priory as a *familiaris*. In addition to continuing to write poetry, Brother Antoninus practiced the art he learned as a young man and set up a priory press, even designing his own typeface. The publication of his collection, *Crooked Lines of God*, brought him national attention, especially in the Catholic community. In great demand as a lecturer and reader of his work Brother Antoninus, in his black and white habit, became a familiar figure on college and university campuses. Everson left the Dominicans in 1969 and married for a third time. The reader can see a marked difference between the poems he wrote while in the Order and those he wrote before and after. Everson was also an expert on the works of Robinson Jeffers and Walt Whitman and wrote extensively about them. William Everson died in 1994 from Parkinson's Disease.

OUT OF THE ASH

Solstice of the dark, the absolute
Zero of the year. Praise God
Who comes for us again, our lives
Pulled to their fisted knot,
Cinched tight with cold, drawn

To the heart's constriction; our faces
Seamed like clinkers in the grate,
Hands like tongs - Praise God
That Christ, phoenix immortal,
Springs up again from the solstice ash,
Drives his equatorial ray
Into our cloud, emblazons
Our stiff brow, dries
Our chill tears. Come Christ,
Most gentle and throat-pulsing Bird!
O come, sweet Child! Be gladness
In our church! Waken with anthems
Our bare rafters! O phoenix
Forever! Virgin-wombed
And burning in the dark,
Be born! Be born!

THE ENCOUNTER

My Lord came to me in the deep of night;
The sullen dark was wounded with His name.
I was as woman made before His eyes;
My nakedness was as a secret shame.
I was a thing of flesh for His despise;
was a nakedness before His sight.

My Lord came to me in my depth of dross;
was as a woman made and hung with shame,
His lips sucked the marrow of my mind,
And all my body burned to bear His name,
Upon my heart He placed His pouring pain;

hung upon Him as the albatross
Hangs on the undering gale and is sustained.

My Lord came to me and I knew, I knew.
I was a uselessness and yet He came
Shafted of the center of the sun.
was a nakedness and was of shame;
was a nothingness and unbegun.
The look He leaned upon me lit me through.

My Lord came to me in my own amaze;
My body burned and that was of my shame.
I who was too impure to meet His gaze
Bent beneath the impress of His name.
He broke beyond the burning and the blame,
And burned the blame to make that pain of praise.

My Lord went from me and I could not be.
I fell through altitudes of leveled light,
As, shaken into space from his mast-tree,
The lookout falls unto the patient sea,
Falling forever through Time's windless flight
To meet the waters of eternity.

Michael Field

Michael Field was actually two poets, both of them women. Katherine Harris Bradley (1846-1914) and her niece, Edith Emma Cooper (1862-1913) used the pseudonym to write poetry and verse drama. The well educated women, who lived together, produced their first joint work in 1884. Their literary friends included Robert Browning and Oscar Wilde. Bradley and Cooper both converted to Catholicism in 1907 and then joined the Third Order of Saint Dominic. Their subsequent works reflect their conversions, whereas their earlier writing was influenced by classical and Renaissance culture. They numbered Father Vincent McNabb among their many Dominican friends. Bradley and Cooper passed away from cancer within a year of each other and both continued to attend daily Mass until a few days before their deaths. Over the years there have been persistent rumors of their lesbianism, but no evidence whatever has been produced.

A Summer Wind

O wind, thou hast thy kingdom in the trees,
    And all thy royalties
    Sweep through the land to-day.
        It is mid June,
And thou, with all thy instruments in tune,
    Thine orchestra
Of heaving fields and heavy swinging fir,
    Strikest a lay
    That doth rehearse
Her ancient freedom to the universe
    All other sound in awe
    Repeats its law:

> The bird is mute; the sea
> Sucks up its waves; from rain
> The burthened clouds refrain,
> To listen to thee in thy leafery,
> Thou unconfined,
> Lavish, large, soothing, refluent summer wind.

DESCENT FROM THE CROSS

Come down from the Cross, my soul, and save thyself –
    come down!
Thou wilt be free as wind. None meeting thee will know
How thou wert hanging stark, my soul; outside the town,
Thou wilt fare to and fro;
Thy feet in grass will smell of faithful thyme; thy head...
Think of the thorns, my soul – how wilt thou cast them off,
With shudder at the bleeding clench they hold!
But on their wounds thou wilt a balsam spread,
And over that a verdurous circle rolled
With gathered violets, sweet and bright violets, sweet
As incense of the thyme on thy free feet;
A wreath thou wilt not give away, nor wilt thou doff.

Come down from the Cross, my soul, and save thyself;
    yea, more
As scudding swans pass blithely on a seaward stream!
Thou wilt have everything thou wert made great to love;
Thou wilt have ease for every dream;
No nails with fang will hold thy purpose to one aim;
There will be arbours round about thee, not one trunk
Against thy shoulders pressed and burning them with hate,

Yea, burning with intolerable flame.
O lips, such noxious vinegar have drunk.

There are through valley-woods and mountain glades
Rivers where thirst in naked prowess wades;
And there are wells in solitude whose chill no hour
      abates!

Come down from the Cross, my soul, and save thyself!
    A sign
Thou wilt become to many as a shooting star.
They will believe thou art ethereal, divine,
When thou art where they are;
They will believe in thee and give thee feasts and praise.
They will believe thy power when thou hast loosed thy nails;
For power to them is fetterless and grand:
For destiny to them, along their ways,
Is one whose earthly kingdom never fails.
Thou wilt be as a prophet or a king
In thy tremendous term of flourishing
And thy hot royalty with acclamation fanned.

Come down from the Cross, my soul, and save thyself!
    . . . Beware!
Art thou not crucified with God, who is thy breath?
Wilt thou not hang as He while mockers laugh and stare?
Wilt thou not die His death?
Wilt thou not stay as He with nails and thorns and thirst?
Wilt thou not choose to conquer faith in His lone style?
Wilt thou not be with Him and hold thee still?
Voices have cried to Him,"Come Down!" Accursed
And vain those voices, striving to beguile!

How heedless, solemn-gray in powerful mass,
Christ droops among the echoes as they pass!
O soul, remain with Him, with Him thy doom fulfill!

Fellowship

In the old accents I will sing, My Glory, my Delight,
In the old accents, tipped with flame, before we knew
    the right
True way of singing with reserve, O Love, with pagan
    might.

White in our steeds, and white too in our armour let us
    ride,
Immortal, white triumphing, flashing downward side by
    side
To where our friends, the Argonauts, are fighting with
    the tide.

Let us draw calm to them. Beloved, the souls on heavenly
    voyage bound,
Saluting as one presence. Great disaster were it found,
If one with half-fed lambency should halt and flicker
    round.

Marionettes

We met
After a year. I shall never forget
How odd it was for our eyes to meet,
For we had to repeat
In our glances the words that we had said
In days when, as our lashes lifted
Or drooped, the universe was shifted.
We had not closed with the past, then why
Did the sense come over us as a fetter
That all we did, speaking eye to eye,
Had been done before, and so much better?
Think - but there's no saying,
What made us so hateful was the rage
Of our souls at finding themselves a stage
Where Marionettes were playing;
For a great actor once had trod
  Those boards, and played the god.

Qui Renovat Juventutem Meam

Make me grow young again,
Grow young enough to die,
That, in a joy unseared of pain,
May my Lover, loved, attain,
With that fresh sigh
Eternity
Gives to the young to breathe about the heart,
Until their trust in youth-time shall depart.

Let me be young as when
To die was past my thought:
And earth with straight immortal men,
And women deathless to my ken,
Cast fear to nought!
Let faith be fraught,
My Bridegroom, with such gallant love, its range
Simply surpasses every halt of change!
Let me come to Thee young,
When thou dost challenge, Come!
With all my marveling dreams unsung,
Their promise by first passion stung,
Though chary, dumb…
Thou callest, Come!
Let me rush to Thee when I pass,
Keen as a child across the grass.

Aridity

O soul, canst thou not understand
Thou art not left alone,
As a dog to howl and moan
His master's absence? Thou art as a book
Left in a room that He forsook,
But returns to by and by,
A book of His dear choice, -
That quiet waiteth for His Hand,
That quiet waiteth for His Eye
That quiet waiteth for His Voice.

Sister Mary Jeremy Finnegan, O.P.

Alice Winifred Finnegan, born in Chicago in 1907, earned a master's degree in English from the University of Chicago where she was a member of Phi Beta Kappa. While at the university she won the John Billings Fiske Prize for Poetry, with Thornton Wilder serving as one of the judges. Finnegan entered the Dominican Sisters at Sinsinawa, Wisconsin in 1932, receiving the name Sister Mary Jeremy. She went on to earn a doctorate in literature from Yale University and in 1942 joined the faculty of Rosary College, River Forest, Illinois. Sister Jeremy's poems appeared in *The Saturday Review of Literature, University of Chicago Magazine, College English, Poetry* and other journals. Her collection, *Dialogue With An Angel,* was praised by critics. She died at Sinsinawa in 1997.

THE CANDLE LIGHTER

DAHLIA-RED, the shadowed curtains
Moved in the dusk and she came through
Holding a simpler rod than Aaron's
Where from a subtler wonder grew;

For every ivory stem she crowned with
Fabulous bursts of daisy-flame,
Bright in the stillness, point and petal,
How fast that angels' Maytime came!

Her leafless, scentless, birdless orchard
Touched walls and roof till they were air,
Blued into mist and clean forgotten;
The winds of peace flowed everywhere.

Still in the midst, the blowing fires
In rows and slants were plain to see;

Grave-eyed, she raised her sceptre higher
And kindled stars upon a tree.

Then watchfires waked the sleeping marches
Of earth and sky with flaring shout
Back from the bounds of miracle
A vast compassion found us out.

We had been pent where lions raved
And basilisks paced to and fro;
Meek now as lambs, with golden eyes
They followed her, and we could go

Beyond the moon and waning Mars,
Behind that seraph changing-rod
Until the farthest suns grew faint
In the excelling light of God.

HOMAGE

MY cool and shadowy sisters like strong trees
Beside deep waters
Your hidden fruit is fragrant beyond thought.

From your deep secret wounds flows balm of patience,
Pungent, and healing pain through all the world.

You make no clamor, none, though tempests shake you
But when the birds from heaven come, low music
Rings in your leaves.

You stand in view of wastelands without water
Making an island of green solitude.

Your secret generation who shall witness?
The island widens imperceptibly
And where you stand, your grave and silent daughters
Shall stand in the world's night as valiantly.

Ruth Mary Fox

Ruth Mary Fox graduated from Saint Clara College, operated by the Dominicans Sisters in Sinsinawa, Wisconsin in 1913. (The college later became Rosary College at River Forest, Illinois.) At Sinsinawa she began a lifelong friendship with the Dominican Sisters which prompted her entrance into the Third Order of Saint Dominic. Ms. Fox went on to teach English at the University of Wisconsin- Milwaukee and to become a renowned scholar of the works of Dante. Her book, *Dante Lights The Way*, published in 1958, was well received by literary critics. After 47 years of teaching, Ms. Fox retired to an apartment on the campus of Edgewood College, operated by the Dominican Sisters in Madison, Wisconsin, because she wanted to live out her life among Dominican religious. During her long life she published poems in *Commonweal*, *English Journal* and the *New York Times*. A collection of her poems, *Some Did Return*, was published after her death in 1976.

OF WORDS

Except a soul there is not anything
That God has made so wondrous as a word,
With which the soul reveals itself when stirred;
Without which never any soul could bring
Thought to another soul, or glorious fling

His thought across far space till nations heard
And ages, and at last the whole world whirred
With his ideas, his word acknowledging.

Yea, and the Father called His only Son
The Word. It was made flesh and dwelt among
Us thirty years, and now each morn my tongue

Receives that living Word. Christ, let not one
Unworthy word ever be born of me
Who has understood a word's high dignity.

WHEN I AT LAST AM COME TO DIE

I longed to live a cloistered life
    Of praise and love and mystic power,
But God has set me in the strife
    Of a tumultuous thoroughfare.

So I have built an anchorhold
    In my own soul, and by and by
I shall forget who bought and sold
    And peacefully shall come to die.

I shall that day be habited
    In Dominic's wool; nuns will be nigh
To chant the Salve round my bed,
    When I at last am come to die.

My cherished wish I know full well
    The Lord I love will not deny;
Himself He'll ring some cloistral bell
    In heaven when I am come to die.

And I shall know them in that hour
    Sweet Gertrude and the Lady Clare,
Imelda and the Little Flower,
    And dear Saint Catherine will be there.

A thousand other nuns there'll be
    Who kept the cloister of the heart
Though here on earth they lived like me,
    In tumult in the busy mart.

And she will hear that Salve ring,
    The Holy Queen who reigns on high
And take my soul to Christ the King,
    When I at last am come to die.

Prayer For The First Day Of School

Send me today students that I can reach.
I do not ask Thee, Lord, that those enroll
With me whose brilliant minds or gifts of soul
Would bring me joy. Send me those I beseech
Who need what I can give. In my work for each
Of them I pray, help me fulfill the whole
Of Thy design, my every thought control:
Then Jesus, Master, teach me how to teach.

If I would really teach, Lord, I must learn
Of Thee, Who on the mount taught the vast throng
The fundamental lessons that belong
To all mankind alike. Then I must turn
To watch Thee drawing single souls apart
To teach Thy finest lessons heart to heart.

Some Did Return

"The undiscovered country from whose bourne No traveler returns."
Hamlet III, Scene 1, 79-80

Ah, but some did return: the widow's son,
The girl Jairus loved, and he for whom
Martha and Mary wept! These Jesus won
Back to mortality, snatched from the tomb.
They did come back. But they have left no word
Of that far country to which we must go
Who never will return. What they have seen and heard
Until we reach that bourne we shall not know.

There must have been a strange light in the eyes
Lit by a soul that had seen heaven and God.
For one who had passed the judgment, great surprise
At things that men call good. He must have trod
The earth an alien. Silent he must be
For want of words who has glimpsed eternity.

Father Francis Augustine Gaffney, O.P.

Francis Gaffney, born in 1863, received the religious name of Augustine when he entered the novitiate of the Dominican Province of Saint Joseph. After ordination he served in a number of parishes in the eastern United States. In addition to his parochial ministry, Father Gaffney wrote over one hundred poems, most of them of a devotional nature or to commemorate religious professions, ordinations, weddings and funerals. In a few of his poems, however, he expressed his strong support for Irish independence. *Sonnets and Other Verses*, published in 1916, is a collection of his works. Father Gaffney died in 1922.

Our Lady of the Rosary

The Lord hath blessed Thee by His power, because by Thee He hath brought our enemies to naught.
— *Judith xiii. 23.*

LEPANTO marks the spot of victory,
O'er crescent cruel and strong, by forces weak,
Of hallowed cross; of which, "if sign you seek,"
'Tis not of man but a Divinity.
The white-robed Pius Fifth the Rosary
Uplifted like the rod of Moses, meek;
Whilst Ottomans on Christians wrath would wreak.
And, as of old, engulfed them in the sea.

O Lady of the Rosary today,
Thy clients all beseech thee, hear their prayer,
And beg the Christ Who raging storms did quell,
Bid warring nations cease their bloody fray;
His power and thine honor, we declare,
O Thou All-Fair, thou joy of Israel.

St. Patrick

APOSTLE, patron Saint of Innisfail!
Akin to Moses, leader of the clans
Of God's own people, with uplifted hands
Obtain swift vict'ry for the struggling Gael!
In Erin quench the heathen fires of Baal.
Implore the God of might that Celtic bands

May thrall of tyrant base and his commands
O'erthrow, and with thy love Hibernia e'er regale.
Thine are our swelling hearts and thine our praise,
And thine the gleaming isle of emerald sheen
Where faith ne'er dies nor dastard craven lives.
Oh be thou comforter! that hours and days,
And years of woe may change to cycles, e'en
Of fullest joy, that Christ-like suffering gives.

A Soggarth's Prayer

Soggarth is the Irish word for priest. Confess is used in the sense of to acknowledge or affirm.

MAY no sin distress thee
    Nor evil oppress thee
Nor sadness possess thee
    And bright be thy way.
May angels caress thee,
And God's Mother bless thee,
And Jesus confess thee -
    The Soggarth will pray.

Father Henry Michael Gaffney, O.P.

Henry Michael Gaffney was born in Ireland in 1895. When he entered the Dominican Order he received the religious name Sylvester although he always wrote under the name Henry. In addition to being a parish priest, Father Gaffney was a poet, playwright and author of short stories, children's books and nonfiction, writing in both English and Gaelic. Active in the Catholic Theatre Society, he wrote numerous plays for religious drama groups. *The Sorrow of the Stars*, published by Talbot Press in 1916, is a collection of his poems previously published in Catholic magazines. Father Gaffney died in 1974.

OUR LADY DREAMS

Mary! I see thy soft, fast-dimming eyes
Abrooding o'er His little, golden head;
Tear-misted eyes that see in vision rise
The terror of the thorns: which see, dull red,
The cruel bruises on that sweet, white brow,
The golden hair blood-clotted—this, thine own,
Thy little Son, thou seest in vision now
Bereft of all His beauty, and alone! . . .
O Mother! My poor tears with thine fall free
To know thy darling little Babe must tread
The wine-press all alone one day for me . . .

In the House of Them That Love Thee

I saw Thee once, O Christ, when I was young,
    In dreams or in my waking hours
I cannot tell. Thou wert, as saints have sung,
    All white and ruddy, Lord, and flowers
Of flaming red engemmed the spotless snow
    Of Thy chaste flesh. I loved Thee then
And whispered to Thee softly, Jesus, low
    Sweet words of innocent love: men
Might leave Thee, but through all the long years I
    Thy very own should be until
The flash resplendent of eternity
    Gave Thee to me forever. Still
My mourning heart remembers now that Thou
    Didst look me sadly in the eyes,
Didst show me Thy poor hands, and tell me how
    These crimson wounds were given. Sighs
Nigh broke Thy gentle voice as Thou didst tell
    Me that these wounds were made in Thee
By them that say they love Thy beauty well!
    "My King!" I say agrieving, "see
Thou hast one lover who will ever cling
    To Thy dear side" ... Too daring vow,
Unknowing what the traitor years would bring!
    I know my coward soul, great King,
I know my faithless heart, more deeply now.

John Gray

John Gray was born in 1864 in a working class neighborhood in London, the son of a carpenter and the first of nine children. He left school at the age of thirteen to apprentice as a metal worker, but continued his education through evening classes, studying French, German and Latin. In 1882 he passed the civil service exam and became a librarian for the Foreign Office. A handsome, intelligent and talented young man who had cultivated fine manners, Gray soon became one of the circle of aesthetic (some said "decadent") writers and artists which included Ernest Dawson, Aubrey Beardsley and Oscar Wilde. Talented in languages, he translated the works of Paul Verlaine, Arthur Rimbaud and other French Symbolists as well as publishing his own poetry. He was widely rumored to have been the inspiration for Oscar Wilde's novel, *The Picture of Dorian Gray*, something John Gray denied. Evidently, however, Wilde was infatuated with him until Wilde turned his affections to Alfred Lord Douglas. Gray converted to Catholicism in 1890, but soon lapsed. Oscar Wilde's trial for gross indecency apparently caused much soul searching in him and he returned to the faith in 1895 and joined the Third Order of Saint Dominic. In 1896 his third book, *Spiritual Poems*, which contained eleven of his own poems and translations of spiritual poets such as Saint John of the Cross, revealed the impact of his conversion. In 1898 at the age of thirty-two he quit his job at the Foreign Office to enter the Scots College in Rome to study for the diocesan priesthood and was ordained in 1901.

Gray's most important supporter and lifelong friend was Marc-Andre Raffalovich, a wealthy French Jewish poet and early writer about homosexuality. Some historians claim that the two men were lovers in their early relationship. Raffalovich, however, wrote that the duty of a homosexual was to overcome and transcend his desires with artistic pursuits and spiritual friendships. Whatever the case, Raffalovich also converted to Catholicism in 1896 and joined the Dominican Third Order and the two men remained close, but apparently chaste, companions until Raffalovich's death a few months before Gray's.

Father Gray's first assignment was to a poor parish in Edinburgh where, according to one writer, he had to contend with near Dickensian poverty. In 1905 he became pastor of the new parish of Saint Peter where the building of the beautiful new church was largely financed by Raffalovich who had settled nearby. Father Gray proved to be a good pastor, establishing a school and the Confraternity of the Rosary. Despite being a busy parish priest, he was able to produce four more books of poetry and a novel. When Father Gray died in 1934, the provincial of the English Dominicans preached a eulogy at his funeral.

A Crucifix
For Ernest Dawson

"Holily dispart" means open in a holy way.

A gothic church. At the end of the aisle,
Against a wall where mystic sunbeams smile
Through painted windows, orange, blue and gold,
The Christ's unutterable charm behold.
Upon the cross, adorned with gold and green,
Long fluted golden tongues of somber sheen,
Like four flames joined in one, around the head
And by the outstretched arms, their glory spread.
The statue is of wood; of natural size;
Tinted; one almost sees before one's eyes
The last convulsion of the lingering breath.
"Behold the man!" Robust and frail. Beneath
That breast indeed might throb the Sacred Heart.

And from the lips, so holily dispart,
The dying murmur breathes "Forgive! Forgive!"
O wide-stretched arms! "I perish, let them live."
Under the torture of the thorny crown,
The loving pallor of the brow looks down
On human blindness, on the toiler's woes;
The while, to overturn Despair's repose,
And urge to Hope and Love, as Faith demands,
Bleed, bleed the feet, the broken side, the hands.

A poet, painter, Christian, — it was a friend
Of mine—his attributes most fitly blend—
Who saw this marvel, made an exquisite
Copy; and knowing how I worshipped it,
Forgot it, in my room, by accident,
I write these verses in acknowledgement.

A Une Madone.
Imitated from the French of Charles Baudelaire

In this poem Gray tells the Madonna that he will build for her a shrine and a statue from his misery and sins and seek hope and forgiveness.

Madone! My lady, I will build thee
A grotto altar of my misery.

Deep will I scoop, where darkest lies my heart,
Far from the world's cupidity apart,

A niche, with mercy stained, and streaked with gold,
Where none thy statue's wonder may behold.

Then, for thy head, I will fashion a tiar,
A filigree of verse, with many a star

Of crystal rhyme its heavy folds upon
And jealousy, O mortal! My Madone,

Shall cut for thee a gown, of dreadful guise
Which, like a portcullis, shall veil thy thighs;

Rude, heavy curtain, faced with bitter fears,
Broidered, in place of pearls, with all my tears

And, of my worship, shoes will I design;
Two satin shoes, to case thy feet divine,

Which, while their precious freight they softly hold,
Shall guard the imprint in a faithful mould.

If I should fail to forge a silver moon,
I with my art, for thee to tread upon,

Then will I place the writhing beast that hangs
Up in my heart, and tears it with his fangs

Where thou may'st crush his head, and smile supreme,
O majesty! All potent to redeem

And all my thoughts, like candles, shall thou see
Before thine altar spread, Star of the Sea!

Starring thine azure roof with points of fire,
With nought but thee to cherish and admire,

So shall my soul in plaintive fumes arise
Of incense ever to thy pitying eyes.

Last, that indeed a Mary thou may'st be,
And that my love be mixed with cruelty—

Of foul voluptuousness! When I have made
Of every deadly sin a deadlier blade,

Torturer filled with pain will I draw near
The target of thy breast, and sick with fear,

Deliberately plant them all where throbs
Thy bleeding heart, and stifling with its sobs.

Father Thomas Heath, O.P.

Thomas Heath, a member of the Province of Saint Joseph, served as a professor of theology, writer, novice master and missionary. Both his brothers Mark and Walter were members of the Order. Besides books and articles in theology, he had poems published in *Sign, Ave Maria* and other Catholic magazines. He was martyred in Kenya in 2005.

ALL SAINTS ALL SOULS

All Saints All Souls, and the wind moans
Above the river for a resting place.
The spirit in me moans above the river of my body.

The trees are emotional women,
Hair streaming, sobbing, sobbing,
And I am frightened and helpless.

The room is cold. I have no fireplace
Or friendly dog or time to waste on poetry,
Or children playing on the rug.

What struggle the saints have had,
The scholar-saints, coming to their desks
And working through such wild emotions.

Thomas Aquinas in Paris on All Saints All Souls
Saw the wind along the Seine, his heart
wisting him to Sicily and the sun.

He put his feet in straw and wrote his straw.
I cannot even concentrate today on what he wrote.
But he heard this wind,

And none can hear it, feel the cold,
See the wild patterns in the branches
Against the sullen sky, and be unmoved.

All Saints All Souls, the Mass in white,
The trees in black. The mind on glory,
The heart on suffering in the pit.

The spirit crying through the viscera
The uselessness of life since all,
All, all, is nothing.

To you I send this helplessness today.
O hope, O life, O warm Sicilian sun.

PRAY FOR ME WHEN I AM DEAD

I do, but feel I am not heard.
My life is not a prayer.
I think of how like me you were.
Your life was not a prayer.

I loved your total shabbiness,
And was that bad or good?
Well, in my beggar's cry that love,
I think, is understood

(I hope, I hope, is understood)

By him whom crying lepers touched,
To whom I touch this prayer.
Who once had shabby friends saves me
From praying in despair.

You That Have No Lines

Father Heath was inspired to write this poem when he gazed out at his students, knowing the pain that life would inevitably bring them, but knowing also that it is useless to tell that to the young.

You that have no lines of former pain,
Nor suffered with the dying, held the dead,
That feel as yet no anguish of insane
Betrayals twisting questions in your head;
That have exams and chatter only: How
The moon shall kiss the planets when he calls;
You cannot hear your answers echo now
Down vaster than these academic halls.
Nor can I make you listen. You will learn
Of this from lectures less conservative,
From sudden storms and flames that smash and burn
Your heart with wounds professors do not give.
I tell you storms will come. You smile and smell
Sweet April, and are restless for the bell.

Father Armando P. Ibáñez, O.P.

Armando Ibáñez, born in Texas in 1949, is a poet, writer and filmmaker. He earned a master of fine arts degree from The American Film Institute and wrote for the *Corpus-Christi Caller-Times* before he entered the Dominican Province of Saint Martin de Porres in 1988. After his ordination in 1993 Father Ibañez served in a variety of ministries including campus minister at Tulane and Stanford Universities and chaplain to the Dominican nuns at the Monastery of the Angels in Hollywood, California.

His first book of poetry, *Midday Shadows*, published in 1980, was followed by *Wrestling With the Angel* in 1997. Father Ibañez writes many of his poems in a unique linguistic style he calls "Tex-Mex" or "Spanglish." He has been published in several journals and has produced a number of poetry videos, some of which have been screened at national and international festivals.

Today he is president, executive producer and director of Pluma Pictures, Inc., a film production company, which he founded, dedicated to making films that espouse universal values.

GENTLENESS

Don't confuse gentleness
With weakness
For all the power of the sea
Is in the mist,
In a snow flake,
In a raindrop.

GRACE

To see with grace
Is seeing
After God removes
An onion skin
From your eyes.

Then we can truly see
What has always been
There to see
God's fingerprints
In all things.

AVE MARIA

Ave Maria
watchful eyes
folded hands
mopping floors

you nursed
the child
son
burped
on your shoulder
jumping
on your lap
gurgling smiles
cooed

prayer
whispered
pleading eyes
hopeful breath
bread

MONASTERY OF THE ANGELS

Faint angel whispers in the breeze
in roses,
in pumpkin bread,
chocolates.
The best kept secret in Hollywood
tucked in folded hands,
behind eyelids
and closed corridors.

Incense,
Birds singing,
spiders knitting,
laughter,
spilt tears on sprouting grass.

Chants,
Rising sun,
Hands upward
Thanking God.
Monastery of the Angels,
Nuns in shadows,
Mouths of fire
Lights the sky.

Prayers of invisible flames
Illuminating, Liberating, Healing –
Christ child upon my lap.

In black on white,
clicking beads,
Hope sweats
with clutching fingertips.
Wisps of dreams,
Years washed away,
Incense rising.

What was,
What could've been,
What is
Is in faint angel whispers.

Mother Rose Hawthorne Lathrop, O.P.

Rose Hawthorne was born in Concord, Massachusetts in 1851, the daughter of writer Nathaniel Hawthorne. She grew up in a literary atmosphere; the hospitable home overflowed with notable writers: Emerson, Melville, Thoreau and Alcott. Young Rose travelled to England, Italy and Germany. In 1871 she married George Parsons Lathrop, a young writer and, for a time, assistant editor of *The Atlantic Monthly*. It seemed like an ideal match; both were writers and both converted to Catholicism, but it was not a happy union. In 1876 their son, Francis, was born, but died at the age of five. Rose sought consolation in her religion; George turned to drink. The couple separated permanently in 1895.

Discovering that her former seamstress had died alone of cancer in a charity hospital changed Rose in a dramatic way. After investigating the fate of poor cancer victims she discovered a new purpose for her life. Inspired by the work of her friend, Emma Lazarus, she took a nursing course, rented a few rooms and began taking in poor people with terminal cancer. Her objective was to make them as comfortable as possible and to allow them to spend their remaining days in a loving environment. Eventually a few other women joined the work. Rose returned to writing to earn money to support her ministry.

The death of George Lathrop from alcoholism in 1898 freed her to form a religious community. In 1900 she and six companions pronounced their vows as Dominican Servants for the Relief of Incurable Cancer, who became known more commonly as the Hawthorne Sisters. She took the name Mother Mary Alphonsa. Mother Hawthorne died in 1927 and the cause for her beatification is being pursued. Her sisters continue her work of caring for the terminally ill.

BEYOND UTTERANCE.

There in the midst of gloom the church-spire rose,
And not a star lit any side of heaven;
In glades not far the damp reeds coldly touched
Their sides, like soldiers dead before they fall;
There in the belfry clung the sleeping bat,
Most abject creature, hanging like a leaf
Down from the bell-tongue, silent as the speech
The dead have lost ere they are laid in graves.

A melancholy prelude I would sing
To song more drear, while thought soars into gloom
Find me the harbor of the roaming storm,
Or end of souls whose doom is life itself!
So vague, yet surely sad, the song I dream
And utter not. So sends the tide its roll,
Unending chord of horror for a woe
We but half know, even when we die of it.

THE SUICIDE.

A shadowed form before the light,
A gleaming face against the night,
Clutched hands across a halo bright
Of blowing hair, - her fixed sight
Stares down where moving black, below,
The river's deathly waves in murmurous silence flow.

The moon falls fainting on the sky,
The dark woods bow their heads in sorrow,
The earth sends up a misty sigh:
A soul defies the morrow!

A Song Before Grief.

Sorrow, my friend,
When shall you come again?
The wind is slow, and the bent willows send
Their silvery motions wearily down the plain.
The bird is dead
That sang this morning through the summer rain!

Sorrow, my friend,
When love and joy are strong,
Your terrible visage from my sight I rend
With glances to blue heaven. Hovering along,
By mine your shadow led,
"Away!" I shriek, "nor dare to work my new-sprung mercies
      wrong!"

Still, you are near:
Who can your care withstand?
When deep eternity shall look most clear,
Sending bright waves to kiss the trembling land,
My joy shall disappear, -
A flaming torch thrown to the golden sea by your pale hand.

Pride: Fate.

Lullaby on the wing
    Of my song, O my own!
Soft airs of evening
    Join my song's murmuring tone.

Lullaby, O my love!
    Close your eyes, lake-like clear;
Lullaby, while above
    Wake the stars, with heaven near.

Lullaby, sweet, so still
    In arms of death; I alone
Sing lullaby, like a rill,
    To your form, cold as a stone.

Lullaby, O my heart!
    Sleep in peace, all alone;
Night has come, and your part
    For loving is wholly done!

FRANCIE.

Francie was Rose Hawthorne's son who died at the age of five.

I loved a child as we should love
    Each other everywhere;
I cared more for his happiness
    Than I dreaded my own despair.

An angel asked me to give him
    My whole life's dearest cost;
And in adding mine to his treasures
    I knew they could never be lost.

To his heart I gave the gold,
    Though little my own had known;

To his eyes what tenderness
    From youth in mine had grown!

I gave him all my buoyant
    Hope for my future years;
I gave him whatever melody
    My voice had steeped in tears.

Upon this shore of darkness
    His drifted body lies.
He is dead, and I stand beside him,
    With his beauty in my eyes.

I am like those withered petals
    We see on a winter day,
That gladly gave their color
    In the happy summer away

I am glad I lavished my worthiest
    To fashion his greater worth;
Since he will live in heaven,
    I shall lie content in the earth.

THE OUTGOING RACE.

The mothers wish for no more daughters;
There is no future before them.
They bow their heads and their pride
At the end of the many tribes' journey.

The mothers weep over their children,
Loved and unwelcome together,
Who should have been dreamed, not born,
Since there is no road for the Indian.

The mothers see into the future,
Beyond the end of that Chieftain
Who shall be the last of the race
Which allowed only death to a coward.

The square, cold cheeks, lips firm-set,
The hot, straight glance, and the throat-line,
Held like a stag's on the cliff,
Shall be swept by the night-winds, and vanish!

Shane Leslie

Sir John Randolph Leslie, third baronet of Glaslough, was born in Castle Leslie, County Monaghan, Ireland in 1885 to an Anglican family. His prominent extended family included his first cousin, Winston Churchill. While a student at King's College, Cambridge, he converted to Roman Catholicism and soon after joined the Third Order of Saint Dominic. About that same time Leslie became a strong supporter of Irish Home Rule and he began using an Irish variant of John—Shane- as his first name. He chose a career in the diplomatic service and helped to negotiate the Anglo-Irish Treaty of 1921. He married Marjorie Ide, an American, in 1912 and fathered three children. Leslie wrote in a wide range of forms over several decades— poetry, novels, biography, literary criticism and translations. In 1922 his friend, F. Scott Fitzgerald, dedicated his first novel, *The Beautiful and Damned*, to Leslie. Shane Leslie died at Castle Leslie in 1971.

IRELAND, MOTHER OF PRIESTS

The fishwife sits by the side
Of her childing bed;
Her fire is deserted and sad,
Her beads are long said;
Her tears ebb and flow with the sea,
Her grief on the years,
But little she looks to the tide,
And little she hears:
For children in springtime play round
Her sorrowing heart,
To win them their feeding she loves
To hunger apart;

Her children in summer she counts
Awhile for her own;
But winter is ever the same,
The loved ones are flown.
Far over the sea they are gone,
Far out of her ken.
They travel the farthest of seas
As fishers of men.
Yet never a word to her sons
To keep them at home,
And never a motherly cry
Goes over the foam;
She sits with her head in her hands,
Her eyes on the flame,
And thinks of the others that played,
Yet left her the same,
With vesture she wove on the loom
Four-coloured to be,
And lanterns she trimmed with her hair
To light them to sea.
Oh, far have the living ones gone,
And farther the dead,
For spirits come never to watch
The fisherwife's bed;
And sonless she sits at the hearth,
And peers in the flame,
She knows that their fishing must come
As ever it came
A fishing that never set home,
But seaways it led,
For God who has taken her sons
Has buried her dead.

FLEET STREET

Fleet Street in London was the location of major British newspapers until the 1980's.

I never see the newsboy run
    Amid the whirling street,
    With swift untiring feet,
To cry the latest venture done,
But I expect one day to hear
    Them cry the crack of doom
    And risings from the tomb,
With great Archangel Michael near;
And see them running from the Fleet
    As messengers of God,
    With Heaven's tidings shod
About their brave unwearied feet.

MI CAREME IN CONNAUGHT

Connaught is a county in the west of Ireland. Mi careme is a French term for the third Thursday in Lent which in many parts of southern Europe was a festive break in the Lenten observances. It was apparently not so in nineteenth century Ireland where the Lenten abstinence included dairy products as well as meat. In this poem the village people wait until the bishop and the local priest are away to celebrate their own mi careme. A splutter *is a spitting or sizzling sound;* praties *are potatoes.*

The Bishop is up at the Synod,
    The priest is gone riding away
So we'll quit from our fasting and weeping
    And give ourselves up to our play.

Too long we are living on praties
    And sea-smelly fish from the bay;
We'll boil up a sliver of bacon
    And butter our bread for the day.

For it's hard to be always out feeding
    On turnips and gruel and hay –
So here is dead meat in a splutter
    And a smell of white milk in the tay!

But God in His Pity forgive us
    If we ate for a while this day,
For the Bishop is gone to the Synod
    And the Curate is out on his grey.

NIGHTMARE

I dreamt that the Heavens were beggared
    And Angels went chanting for bread,
That the Cherubs were sewed up in sackcloth
    And Satan anointed his head!

I dreamt they had chalked up a price
    On the Sun and the Stars at God's feet,
And the Devil had bought up the Church
    And put out the Pope in the street!

Sister Mary Benvenuta Little, O.P.

Sister Mary Benvenuta (Dorothy I. Little), an English contemplative nun of All Souls Priory, Headington, Oxford, published three collections of her poems. In addition she translated the Eucharistic meditations of St. John Vianney and was a frequent contributor to the journal, *Blackfriars*. The poems here are from her book, *The Month and Other Poems*, 1921.

Hawkesyard

Hawkesyard was the house of studies of the student brothers of the English Dominican Province. In this poem Sister Benvenuta plays with the name, Hawkesyard, and compares the young friars to fledgling hawks or falcons waiting to be unleashed to capture souls. She uses the terminology of falconry. A mew *is a cage for hawks or falcons –* hawkesyard. *A* jess *is a short strap fastened around the leg of the bird – monastic observances. And* hood *refers both to the capuce of the habit and the leather head covering of the eagerly waiting birds.*

This is the mew of God set high
    Beneath the heavens' windy rafter,
Whence all His falconry shall fly,
And, clean of wing and clear of eye,
    Make sport to wake the angels' laughter.
    Ah, birds of God,
    What prey shall ye bring home hereafter?

Here, hooded by His hand they sit,
    Nor fear the due monastic jesses
That leash them to His wrist, and knit
Their wills to His, as should befit
    The fledglings of His tendernesses,

> Who shall repay
Some day this spring-time of caresses.

Easter Thought

If Paradise be yet more fair
> Than earth in tender April guise,
Poor soul, how shall thy frailty bear
> God's great and ultimate surprise?
Into a thousand fragments there
> Thou needs must break beneath His eyes.

But since in shadow of His face -
> The which is light - death holds no sway,
The fragments, fraught with quickening grace,
> Shall turn to birds that wing their way
With flight more swift than eye can trace
> By laggard light of earthly day.

Some through the trees on every side
> From bough to blossomed bough shall dart,
Some shall in Mary's bosom bide,
> Some in glad carols bear their part;
But oh, the most, the most shall hide,
> A homing flock, within the Heart
Of Jesus Who was crucified.

Domini Canes

This poem is a play on the words Dominicans and Domini Canes, Latin for dogs of the Lord. It refers to a legend that, before St. Dominic's birth, his mother saw a vision of a black and white dog with a torch in his mouth setting the world on fire.

WHEN Hell's wild warriors rode the world rough-shod,
Men's angel guardians drooped their wings and wept;
    And sins that once in dusky by-ways crept
Now on the highroads loud in triumph trod.
Earth seemed subservient to the devil's nod;
    But while His very friends like sluggards slept,
    Forth from the flaming Heart of Love there leapt,
Unleashed by Mary's hands, the Hounds of God.

Great Dominic, star-haloed, heads the pack,
    Deep-mouthed, melodious, hunting down their prey
    Of human souls in house and field and street;
Until the heavenly Huntsman call them back
    With death's clear horn, to lie at close of day
    Beneath her mantle's fold, at Mary's feet.

Father Damian Magrath, O.P.

Damian Magrath was born in Bradford, England and entered the Dominican Order in 1936. From 1948 until his death in 1982 he ministered in South Africa where he taught theology, wrote theological articles and poems and served in provincial administration. His poems were published as *Poems: When Time and Meaning Are One*.

CREATION

The black waves surged,
and merged,
and urged each other on
in a dark night;
endlessly extending to no purpose,
losing their identity scarcely born;
moved by hidden powers thrusting to the surface,
a vast, empty waste, deserted and forlorn.

A stillness,
a silence out of nothing
as if a world were waiting:
listening without ears
as if to hear;
 seeing without sight
 the night;
 breathing without breath
out of death.

Over the face of the deep
a silent ripple leaped,

moved by a gentle breeze,
by a faint breath seized;
moving, hovering,
brooding, covering;
scarcely a sigh,
hardly a murmur,
seeming to die.

As if inhaled
to gather force
within its source,
it came again;
stronger, longer,
bolder, louder,
forming a word,
shaping a sound
that could be heard;

Let there be
over the sea;
sun-bright
moon-light,
star-spark
cleaving the dark;
day and night.
And so it was.

Let there be
out of the sea;
land's features,
living creatures,
sea's surf,

face of earth
brought to birth.
And so it was.

Lux de Caelo Natus Est Nobis

We are always walking in the dark
thinking it is daylight
not seeing what we do not see.

We are always opening our eyes
to the dawn of an horizon where the sun sets as we approach
blind leaders of the blind deceived by sight.

We need to turn around to the true light
which we think is darkness,
to see without seeing
through the eyes of another,
to walk towards that horizon
holding hands like lovers.

All will be well...

Made Flesh

What was it like –
      your entry into time,
to be a child of man
      as well as son of God?

what was it like –

to feel and touch
      and taste the world you made,
depend on Mary's womb
      to come and dwell with us?
what was it like –

to search for shelter in the dark
      be born in straw of manger stark,
o feel the cold, the wind, the rain,
      to see the sun, the moon and stars,
what was it like?

How intimate for you
      to come unto your own
with flesh and blood and bone,
      a human tongue to talk
hands to touch and feet to walk
      a human heart to beat?

Did you not find it strange
      you who did not change
to empty yourself to be like us
      showing your human yearning thus,
did you not find it strange?

Stranger still for us to see
      the body's articulation:
skeletal frame and a human brain to think
      the thoughts of God!

      fleshed in muscle, sinew, nerve;

blood's stream
    life's heartland,
organs' coordination;
    elements built up
into the mystery of life:
    the beauty of pulsating matter,
strange, familiar, body
Stranger still to see its ills
    and love it in its weakness:
shattered, bloody, crushed,
    ill at ease, eaten into,
corrupting, dying;
    to pity its mortality
and love it in its pain;
    strange it is for us.

The health and healing which we serve
    reading with insight the body's tale,
story of muscle, bone and nerve
    fulfills in prophecy the promise:
for in the memory splendor glows
    the immortality of risen flesh,
the proclamation of its healing
    by the son of man.

THE WASHING OF THE FEET

Under Simon's stare
and the company's glare
I, a woman of the city
washed your feet.

Washed them with my tears
repentant of the years,
I, a woman who was a sinner
from off the street.

Wiped them with my hair,
showed that I could care,
I, a daughter of joy
did thus you greet.

Covered them with balm,
lest they came to harm,
I, a woman of the city
washed your feet

He looked on me and I was moved,
moved as I had never been before:
moved by a love I had never felt,
a love that caused my heart to melt;
a love that reached my very core
and in my heart an opening tore

It was a love that said to me:
"I made you for myself,
and my heart is restless
till it rests in thee."

"I loved you in your shame,
I loved you in your fame:
beyond all sins love does atone:

> Did I not fashion you?
> Did I not make you?

    Did I not form you?
    Did I not create you?

"Are you not my mind's delight
ever wondrous in my sight?
Are you not my heart's own treasure
 made in beauty for my pleasure?
Are you not my love's own creature
reflecting me in every feature?"

    "You have yearned,
    and turned,
    and earned
    to be forgiven
because you have been loved much."

Theodore Maynard

Theodore Maynard was born in 1890 in Madras, India where his parents were serving as Salvation Army officers. He attended school in England and began to write for publication—poetry, reviews and essays. In 1913 he converted to Catholicism and shortly after entered the Dominican novitiate at Woodchester, but left after seven months. Maynard cherished his time in the novitiate, however, as can be seen in his poem, *At Woodchester*. After leaving the novitiate he joined the Third Order of Saint Dominic. In 1920 he married Sarah Casey, herself a novelist and playwright, and together they had seven children. In 1921 financial difficulties necessitated his going to teach at Dominican College of San Rafael, California. Although Maynard never fully adjusted to life in the United States and often pined for England, the need for employment kept him in America. He taught at several universities, including Georgetown, Fordham, the Catholic University of America and Saint John's. Maynard wrote widely in poetry, biography and history. One of his most prominent books was *The Story of American Catholicism* (1941). Among his other works is *A Fire Was Lighted*, the biography of another Dominican poet, Mother Rose Hawthorne. Maynard's later years were fraught with more financial difficulties, depression and tuberculosis. He died in 1956.

At Woodchester

HARK how a silver music falls
Between these meek monastic walls,
And airy flute and psaltery
Awaken heavenly melody!

Yet not to unentuned ears
May come the joyance of the spheres,
And only humbled hearts may see
The humble heart of mystery.

Where tread in light and lilting ways
Bright angels through the dance's maze
On grassy floors to meet the just
In robes of woven diamond dust.

And jeweled daisies burst to greet
The flutter of the Blessed's feet:
Along the cloister's gathered gloom
Lilies and mystic roses bloom.

Grown in the hush of hidden hours
Thoughts fairer than the summer flowers
Lift up their sweet and living heads,
Crystalline whites and sanguine reds!

Who keep in lowly pageantry
Silence a lovely ceremony;
Who set a seal upon their eyes
Responsive only to the skies;

Who in a quick obedience move
Along the hallowed paths of love,
Win at last to that secret place
Adorned with the glory of God's face.

And as each eve the tired sun
Sinks softly down, the long day done,
Upon the bosom of the west –
So, even so, upon God's breast

Each weary heart is folded deep
Into His arms in quiet sleep,
And sheltered safe, all warm and bright,
Against the phantoms of the night.

JUDAS

His secret sin
Like cancer burrowed in,
Till naught was left of hale or whole
In all his stricken, tangled soul.

Strange, terrible
Was that descent to hell
When the prim keeper of the bag
Found his accounts began to lag!

Shamed, desperate
His trust to vindicate,
e veiled a small dishonesty
By an enormous treachery.

How cheaply priced
By him his Brother, Christ!
or he who, asking, could have got
Three hundred gold coins, asked them not.

He sought no more
Than tally for his score;
Scrupulous to conceal his loss,
He sent Christ thorn-crowned to the cross!

IN DOMO JOHANNIS
In the house of John

HERE rest the thin worn hands which fondled HIM,
    The trembling lips which magnified the Lord,
Who looked upon His handmaid, the young, slim
    Mary at her meek tasks, and here the sword
Within the soul of her whose anguished eyes
    Gazed at the stars which watch Gethsemane,
And saw the sun fail in the stricken skies.
    In these dim rooms she guards the treasury
Of her white memories - the strange, sweet face
    More marred than any man's, the tender, fain
And eager words, the wistful human grace,
    The mysteries of glory, joy and pain,
And that hope tremulous, half-sob, half-song,
    Ringing through night - "How long, O Lord,
    how long?"

After Communion

NOW art Thou in my house of feeble flesh,
    O Word made flesh! My burning soul by Thine
Caught mystically in a living mesh!
    Now is the royal banquet, now the wine,
The body broken by the courteous Host
    Who is my humble Guest - a Guest adored
Though once I spat upon, scourged at the post,
    Hounded to Calvary and slew my Lord!

My name is Legion, but separate and alone;
    Wash, wash, dear Crucified, my Pilate hand!
Rejected Stone, be Thou my corner-stone!
    Like Mary at the cross's foot I stand;
Like Magdalene upon my sins I grieve;
    Like Thomas do I touch Thee and believe.

Viaticum

DEAR God, not only do Thou come at last
    When death hath filled my heart with dread affright,
But when in gathered dark I meet aghast
    The mimic death that falls on me at night.

The daily dying, when alone I tread
    The valley of the shadow, breast the Styx,
With shrouded soul and body stiff in bed . . .
    And no companion from the welcome pyx!

How should I face disarmed and unawares

    The phantoms of the Pit oblivion brings
My will surrendered, mind unapt for snares,
    Eyes blinded by the evil, shuddering wings,

Did not the sunset stand encoped in gold
    For priestly offices, 'mid censers swung,
And with anointed thumb and finger hold
    The symbolled Godhead to my eager tongue?

Then with my body's trance there doth descend
    Peace on my eyelids, goodness that shall keep
My wandering feet, and at my side a friend
    Through all the winding caverns of my sleep.

MEEKNESS

UPON the Cross, as on a bed,
He lay; and not a word He said--
A lamb as to the slaughter led.

    What pride can stand against such meekness?
    What strength can overthrow such weakness?

"Thy will not mine accomplished be"
But more than pain accepted He
Between the thieves on Calvary.

    His loneliness and dereliction
    Is Agony's complete perfection.

Then rang across the fearful sky
The blasphemous and bitter cry,

Lama, Lama Sabacthanai!

> Darkened the sun; the moon was shaken
> To see their God by God forsaken.

For never since the world began
Had God forsaken any man
Till Christ was laid beneath His ban –

> When by the Father unbefriended
> The stricken Son to hell descended.

No consolation could He have
Who bore our sins our souls to save,
Who passed, unanswered, to the grave.

> What pride can stand against such meekness?
> What strength can overthrow such weakness?

TRAGEDY

Pity the hippopotamus!
Ugly enough he looks to us,
And yet the hide that plates each part
Purses a very tender heart.

An aching heart - or why those eyes
Complaining to the cruel skies
That, though he longs, he has no hope
To leap the nimble antelope?

Birds perch upon him. On what wings
Dare he aspire? And radiant things

Strut, bloom and flash by the river side:
His finest instincts are denied.

Though vast his skull, his wits are dim:
No irony can comfort him,
Nor can he ease his aching heart
By turning anguish into art.

BALLADE OF A FEROCIOUS CATHOLIC

THERE is a term to every loud dispute,
    A final reckoning I'm glad to say:
Some people end discussion with their boot;
    Others, the prigs, will simply walk away.
But I, within a world of rank decay,
    Can face its treasons with a flaming hope,
Undaunted by faith's foemen in array
    I drain a might tankard to the Pope!

They do not ponder on the Absolute,
    But wander in a fog of words astray.
They have no rigid creed one can confute,
    No hearty dogmas riotous and gay,
But feebly mutter through thin lips and grey
    Things foully fashioned out of sin and soap; -
But I, until my body rests in clay,
    I drain a mighty tankard to the Pope!

I've often thought that I would like to shoot
    The modernists on some convenient day;
Pull out eugenists by their noxious root;

    The welfare-worker chattering like a jay
    I'd publicly and pitilessly slay
With blunderbuss or guillotine or rope,
    Burn at the stake, or boil in oil, or flay
I drain a mighty tankard to the Pope!

Prince, proud prince Lucifer, your evil sway
Is over many who in darkness grope:
But as for me, I go another way –
I drain a mighty tankard to the Pope!

Sister Mary Stanislaus McCarthy, O.P.

Sister Mary Stanislaus McCarthy died in 1897 at the age of only 48 years, 30 of them spent as a Dominican Sister of Sion Hill, Blackrock, County Dublin, Ireland. She followed in the literary footsteps of her father, well known poet Denis Florence McCarthy. Sister Mary Stanislaus employed her writing talent only occasionally, however, to commemorate events in the lives of her sisters, students and friends. She placed little value on her verses. After her death friends collected her poems and published them as *Songs of Sion* (1898).

AN ORANGE LEAF

This poem commemorates the orange tree that grows in the garden of the Priory of Santa Sabina in Rome, the motherhouse of the Dominican Friars. Tradition relates that the tree was grown from a series of shoots from a tree planted by Saint Dominic.

AN orange leaf! Six hundred years and more
    Since Dominick, our great patriarch and chief,
      First set the ancient, hallowed tree that bore
        That orange leaf.
So through the ages, spite of unbelief,
    And waning love and persecution's roar,
      Stands the great Order that he set of yore
In Augustinian soil; - and so in brief
    A type art thou of us and many more
        Dear orange leaf!

Napoleon's Happiest Day.

ONE who had reached the zenith of his fame -
Kings and their kingdoms trembled when he frowned -
Was asked, by them who cringing stood around,
His brightest day, his gladdest hour to name.
Without a moment's pause the answer came —
    Some day of conquest, loud with trumpet's sound?
    Some day of civic triumph laurel-crowned?
None such may that proud appellation claim.

"My First Communion Day," he brief replied,
    "That was the happiest day I ever knew."
And then, as answer so unlooked-for tied
    The tongues of all that vapid, worldly crew,
He murmured to himself, and, smiling, sighed:
    "Then I was young, and life seemed good and true."

Father Vincent McNabb, O.P.

The little friar whose reputation ranged from "mad as a hatter" to "the saint of Hyde Park," was born Joseph McNabb in Belfast, Northern Ireland in 1868, one of eleven children. At the age of eighteen he entered the Dominican novitiate at Woodchester, England and received the name Vincent. After studies in Louvain, Belgium and ordination he began teaching at the Dominican House of Studies at Hawkesyard. The provincial assigned him to London in 1920, officially to do parochial work, but it was his preaching and public disputations in Hyde Park for which he became famous. Father McNabb took on all comers—hecklers, atheists, free thinkers, Protestants, intellectuals and literary figures such as George Bernard Shaw. He became a familiar site in London, wearing his habit everywhere (not then the custom in England) because he said Englishmen needed to be reminded of God.

In addition to his poems he produced over ninety books, pamphlets and articles. Along with Eric Gill, Desmond Chute and others he founded the Dominican Third Order community of craftsmen at Ditchling. Known as much for his eccentric ways as for his holiness and preaching, he disdained modern inventions, refused to use a typewriter and insisted on wearing a home spun habit. He seldom used the bed or chair in his room, preferring to sleep on the floor and to read either standing up or kneeling. Father McNabb died in 1943.

Unto the Olive Hill

THOU makest suffering a flower: -
    The cheeks, a pink; a rose, thy lips
Whose dews the song-parched skylark sips.
Thou wearest suffering as a flower.

Thou makest suffering a scent
    Of orchard floor and fresh-turned sod
    And salt sea-ways that stretch to God.
Thou stillest suffering as a scent.

Thou makest suffering a song: -
    A paean of great victory,
    An ode of thy soul's bridal day.
Thou singest suffering as a song.

Thy weakness, Loved, is unto power;
    For Christ, Who smote Death on the tree,
    Hath taught thee His high artistry
To make pain sing, and scent and flower.

Saint Thomas

ANGEL, in mind and heart, thy fervent soul
    Was filled with love and high poetic song.
    Peopling thy fancy, dwelt a mighty throng
Of harmonies divine. Thou could'st control
Such floods of heavenly minstrelsy as roll
    Through minds angelic. Swiftest glance among
    The things of God inspired thee. High and long

Thou chanted'st Panges - anthems sweet that stole
Men's hearts for God. Say then, bard of Christ hid,
How thou could'st limn God, the All-Fair? How press
Jesu's pierced side, th'ensanguined wounds caress
Of Christ, tearless and songless; how forbid
Thy heart its throbs - its rue, lest Truth divine
Should stain its limped rills with ought of thine?

A GOLDEN JUBILEE.

Be still, my soul; and let thy fingers tell
    Once more the thin-worn chaplet of thy years.
I know not Jesus knows - if all be well,
    Or if my willfulness still stirs His tears.

I know with joy the chaplet of my life,
    The fifty golden years His love has lent,
Have been no day of hate-o'ershadowed strife
    But spring-time, with its sunshine and its scent.

With thanks I see across the broad, white, ways
    Of Dominic, wherein my feet have trod,
Not the blurred traces of a lamb that strays,
    But myriad mercies at the feet of God.

Wondering, I feel within this ageing heart
    Some windows close thro'which earth sends
        her chills,
And some new-opened where, from noise apart,
    I stand to hail far-off th' eternal hills.

At such an autumn even-tide I miss
    The spring-morn friendships of a day long dead.
Then 'twas the earth that gave us perfect bliss;
    To-day I visit them in heaven instead.

Whilst bravely telling o'er the fifty years
    I've stood within the furrow of the Lord,
Not in His sternest words I find my fears,
    But in my words and life, that scant accord.

And when so many of earth's pillars, low
    Have fall'n, and are mingling with the dust,
Not in such shadows, but in Him I know,
    (Tho' hid 'neath shadows infinite), I trust.

To Him alone I offer up my praise;
    My timid fledgeling thanks for all He wrought
And bore - so unrepentant in His ways
    Of selling mercy cheaper than He bought.

Give me, O God, to-day at even-tide,
    The waste days of my life to rise above
In perfect trust; and what remains beside
    To consecrate to Thee in perfect love.

Dark Speech upon the Harp

'Lord Jesus, the one whom Thou lovest is sick"
(Jn 11:3).

The one whom Thou lovest is strayed.
I have lost Thee.
I cannot find Thee.
Find me.
Seek me.
I cannot find Thee.
I have lost my way.
Thou art the Way.
Find me, or I am utterly lost.
Thou lovest me.
I do not know if I love Thee;
but I know Thou lovest me.
I do not plead my love, but Thine.
I do not plead my strength, but Thine.
I do not plead my deed, but Thine.
The one whom Thou lovest is sick.
My sickness is that I do not love Thee.
That is the source of my sickness which is approaching death,
I am sinking.
Raise me.
Come to me upon the waters.
Lord Jesus, "the one whom Thou lovest is sick."

Father Paul Murray, O.P.

Paul Brendan Murray was born in Newcastle, County Down, Northern Ireland in 1947. In 1966 he joined the Irish Dominican Province and was ordained a priest in 1973. Since 1994 Father Murray has taught the literature of the mystical tradition at the Pontifical University of Saint Thomas Aquinas (The Angelicum) in Rome. In addition to many works in theology, he has produced three volumes of poetry: *Ritual Poems (1971), Rites and Meditations (1982)* and *The Absent Fountain (1992).* He is also the author of *T.S. Eliot and Mysticism: the Secret History of the Four Quartets.*

SECOND YOUNGEST

My hair still dripping wet
after the bath and with, at last,
the large white towel which had
hung over my shoulders
now in his hands
thought, as I knelt on the ground
before my father
and he dried my hair and talked,
I was the son of a god.

It was the same
warmth, the same repeated ritual
for all of us, my four brothers
and my three sisters –
when, in turn, after our bath
we would climb
the dark stairs to the lighted room
where my father sat in his chair.

We were, I suppose, like small
initiates: the girls
in their coloured night-gowns
and red slippers, and the boys
with our white towels
across our shoulders, wearing pyjamas
but naked from the waist up.

No pilgrims of the Absolute,
it's clear, no shining devotees
in saffron ever looked
as radiant and cleansed as we did
or ever climbed
to their illumined states of soul
as we climbed up those stairs!

I was five or at most
six years old, the second youngest.
But once I had
braved the darkness of the stairs
alone, my trial was over.
From shadows into light
the door opened, and I stepped
into the hush of the room.

So vivid, I remember, that bright
threshold! But real
illumination came, moments
later, when I knelt down
next to the fire, as near
as I could to my father's chair,
and bowed my head.

I remember, as soon
as he began to dry my hair
with the towel
and warm my hair with his hands
lifting his two palms
to the fire
and letting them rest on my head.

I thought I was the son of a god.

THE FIRST WISDOM

Beautiful
are the texts of the Masters,
luminous and practical
their teaching.

But for me
more useful still,
my best-thumbed pages
of enlightenment

and the text and title
of my greatest learning,
are my own
faults and failings.

THRESHOLD

Not at the pointed
hour of ecstasy
or at the furthest edge
of being
but here, in the even
close-knit hours
among the weekday
goings-on
of wind and weather,
here in our hidden threshold
of perception,
here we must wait
until the doors of the present
swing open
on new hinges.

IN THE MAKING

The gift, when it comes,
comes always where
you least expect: either
from that hurt void you feel
after actual loss
or from the mere absence
of a longed-for music,
from a line or a theme
you cannot seem to recall

or the phrase of a poem
you cannot complete.
But then with an instinct
born from that lack
or that need — suddenly
out of the side
of the poem, another music
begins, another song.
And there it is on its feet,
bone of your bone and yet
free, flesh of your flesh
but not years, a theme
like a new Eve emerging.

Hilary Pepler

Douglas Clarke Pepler, born in 1878, was an English printer, writer and puppeteer and also a close associate of Father Vincent McNabb. Along with Eric Gill, Desmond Chute and Father McNabb he founded the Catholic community of craftsmen at Ditchling, Sussex in 1920. Raised a Quaker, Pepler converted to Catholicism in 1916 and soon after became a member of the Third Order of Saint Dominic and founded Saint Dominic's Press. After joining the Third Order he used his religious name, Hilary, exclusively. In addition to printing and writing, he was an avid puppeteer and wrote numerous religious plays for marionettes. Pepler married in 1904 and fathered six children. His son, David, married Gill's daughter. Another son, Conrad, joined the Dominican Friars and for many years ran the Dominican Conference Centre in Stratfordshire. Hilary Pepler died in 1951.

THE LAW THE LAWYERS KNOW ABOUT

The law the lawyers know about
    Is property and land;
But why the leaves are on the trees,
And why the winds disturb the seas,
Why honey is the food of bees,
Why horses have such tender knees,
Why winters come and rivers freeze,
Why Faith is more than what one sees,
And Hope survives the worst disease,
And Charity is more than these,
    They do not understand.

Father Peter Pius Portier, O.P.

Peter Philip Potier was born in London in 1756 into a Catholic family. In 1764 his parents sent his brother and him to Bornham College, operated by Dominican Friars in Belgium, so that they could receive a Catholic education, something not then available in England. In 1773 he entered the Dominican novitiate, receiving the name Pius. Following ordination he taught at Bornham College, but after eleven years he returned to England to minister to Catholics and to help restore the Order there. Father Potier served two terms as provincial of the restored English province and strongly opposed the establishment of the American Province of Saint Joseph. Potier wrote verse, mostly of a doctrinal, moral or devotional nature. His collection, *Fugitive Pieces*, published in 1824, received a negative reception from critics. It is difficult to know whether Father Potier intended some of the humor that modern readers may find in his work. When the publisher of his collection asked him for a dedication he wrote " I cannot flatter; I will not lie, so dedication none have I." In the preface, which he also apparently did not want to do he wrote " I understand that it is generally a rule for every author . . . to bore the public with the vagaries of his brain." Father Potier died in 1846 at the age of ninety.

To Modesty

O Modesty! celestial fair,
With downcast eyes and timid air,
The damask rose is on your cheek,
And all your whole deportment meek;
You move along with decent grace,
No affectation in your pace,

No mincing step, no tiptoe tread,
No twisting, twirling of the head;
No gaping for the applause of fools,
Propriety your motions rules.
You formerly with special care,
Watch'd o'er the toilet of the fair,
Prepar'd their decent plain attire,
Which taste correct will e'er admire;
But they have turn'd you now away,
And shameless bow to fashion's sway.
And since they have discarded you,
They blush not to expose to view
The naked shoulders, breasts quite bare,
'Tis that attracts the dandy's stare;
(The dandy, that disgrace to man,
Beneath the grinning monkey's clan.)
Oh, how the heart with nausea wambles!
When, (quite exposed, as 'twere in shambles
For sale) we see so plump and fresh,
The shoulders, breasts of woman's flesh.
Disgusting sight! fie, woman fie!
Call back discarded Modesty,
That she your toilet may attend
Once more – for she's your kindest friend.

Father Christopher Renz, O.P.

Christopher Renz, born in New Jersey in 1959, received a Ph.D. in microbiology from Northwestern University and did medical research before entering the Dominican Province of the Holy Name in 1989. While a student brother he co-founded The Power of Poetry, a group of poets at the Graduate Theological Union in Berkeley, California. Later he served as editor of *Ruah: A Journal of Spiritual Poetry*. Father Renz was ordained a priest in 1997. Since 2000 he has served on the faculty of the Dominican School of Theology and Philosophy in Berkeley, specializing in spirituality & poetry and theology & science. His poems have appeared in *Ruah, Review for Religious* and *Cresset*. In addition to his poetry, he has published articles about spirituality, liturgy and science.

LAUDS

Beginning just before dawn
there is a clamor
an almost manic clip-clap
of song and wing.
In these last moments,
anxious for night to end
birds whirring at the shadows.

We, too, hope to herald morning:
processing down the corridor to lauds
our long robes flapping at the darkness
open mouths forming a tone poem of light,

The earth holds us,
our movement (the rustle of fear)
our song (the swell of hope)

holds us carefully
and waits (with use)
for the rising sun to speak.
Hush little ones, hush . . .

Lauds
This is Father Renz's second version of "Lauds."

Mist
rising up from clay bricks –
Psalms
I collect
in cupped hands and
raise high,
beseeching the sun.

"Evaporate my life
  into this blue morning,
make of me a swirling praise
  before I disappear into
  the empty space

  between my fingers."

SOIL IN AUTUMN

In late October
I move bulbs, roots
soil, and rock.
I create height and depth
secret hiding places of
color and fragrance.

I am agitated
like soil in autumn.

I turn myself over and over,
dig deeply. I have spent days
putting this place to sleep,
burying my stories
Offering them to
the winter frost
and her darkness.

Will anything survive?

Father Dominic Rover, O.P.

Born in Washington, D.C. in 1920, Thomas Rover left the Georgetown University Law School to enter the Dominican Province of Saint Joseph where he received the name Dominic. After ordination Father Rover taught theology at the Dominican House of Studies and Providence College. He served as confessor and spiritual director to many, was a sought after retreat preacher and a prolific writer. Besides his works in theology, he wrote three plays that were produced at the Blackfriars Guild in New York and a series of television dramas for *The Catholic Hour* for NBC. Father Rover died from Parkinson's Disease in 1998.

ARS MORIENDI: The Art Of Dying

In the late 1970's Father Rover was diagnosed with Parkinson's Disease, an incurable progressive neurological disorder, that eventually killed him. He composed this poem in the early 1980's when he was in the early stage of the disease.

My little finger is dying
   just the tip of the little finger
      of my left hand

I carry my secret carefully
  let it hang like a single gold coin
  in a cluster of other fingers
  still trying to
      stay alive
But the word is out
  and they will have to be ready too
  when their time comes

My Chinese lady-doctor
  who does not believe in acupuncture
    diagnoses my ailment
  in impeccable Latin:
  "Digitus nervix immobilis,"
    which means, of course,
  "Your little finger is dying."

Numb and heavy now
  it will spread like a stain
    of invisible ink
      into the other fingers
    of my left hand,
      down my left arm
      across my chest
      then up the right arm
      into the fingers
      of my right hand:
a lovely rainbow of death.

I am told the dying process
  may skip across the torso for awhile
  if I take hot baths and long walks
    and eat lots of garlic

But infallibly, like fall of night,
  it will descend
    into the nether limbs
    hip to thigh to ankle
      until my feet, hanging there
      in my black Wallabees, wait
        to be declared officially dead!

But I promise:
I will leave my liver to the liver-bank
my kidneys to the kidney-bank
my eyeballs to the eyeball-bank
   and my meager monthly salary
       in perpetuity
   to the Committee for the
       Rehabilitation
       of Downtown Providence

Fully awake now
I notice that all sounds
       and sights and tastes
       are keener…brighter…
I admit that I am jealous
I am jealous because I have never had
       a near-death experience
But I have been near life so many times,
I have felt the touch of life
       and have trembled at the touch
So even in the face of death
       I am willing and eager
       to testify on behalf of life

But I need more time
       there is never enough time
       and death robs us
       of the little that is left
I have work to do
       friends to be loved
       enemies to be forgiven
       words to be shouted against the storm
       shadows to be dispelled

>   that still blot out the sun!

Besides, I am bound by a pact
I made long ago with Beauty
>   that before I died
>   I would shape one word
>   one cry, one song
and let the sound of it reach everywhere
so that no one might escape from love
I cannot describe the power of this word
>   but the thought
>   of bringing it to life in my life
>   fills me with joy

Now, after the word of life
>   there will be time for death
I have made my plans
>   eyes closed, hands folded on my lap
I will lean back in my black vinyl Lazy-Boy
>   and fall like a sash weight
No need for choice or effort
>   or good intentions
The weight of my body
>   will carry me down…down
>   to the place of rest
>   without pain or passion
>   I will give myself over …

According to our custom
>   my body lay overnight
>   in the silence of the House Chapel
>   stretched out in the very place
>   where I used to pray

No, I will not go
    like Howard Hughes
I will cut my hair
    and clip my nails
    and stay clean and neat
    till the very end

I will not, like Damon Runyan
asked to be cremated
and to have my ashes strewn
    lovingly, by helicopter,
over Manhattan Island.
With my luck
a brisk wind
    would come up
        off Sandy Hook
and blow me to Bridgeport

No! I will not imitate anyone
    I will go in my own way,
    covered with unhealed wounds
        uncanceled debts
        and no collateral –
        heavy to look at
        with my heavy hands
        and heavy limbs
        but easy…easy to carry

Lying there I will begin
    to dream about the end –
water all around me
cool and sweet to the lips
One dream recurs

I am a child,
suddenly a child again
let loose after hours
in a Baskin-Robbins Ice-Cream Parlor
free to sample
all thirty-five delicious flavors
O creamy eschaton!

I wore a borrowed Cappa
    and a new pair of shoes
    bought just for the occasion
    plus a large Rosary
      locked in once and for all
      under my rigid hands

I lay there through the night
    and watched my brothers and friends
    as they watched me
    baffled by the choices
    they were free to make
    Should they offer me honor, respect
    puzzlement or honest complaint
    at promises unfulfilled, our common woe?
They watched me carefully and courteously
still wondering who I really was
still wondering too what it would be like to die

I know that I wanted to tell them
    that death always defends its own secrets
      that it always favors darkness
      that it feeds on faith
      and the rush of heart to heart
      (you want to be with the one you love)

      whatever the shape or color of their gaze
      I knew they always looked kindly upon me
      and I know they will be kind to my sisters
      and even lie a little on my behalf –
          to enhance the memory
          of my piety and usefulness

Now there is only my body
      and the place it occupies in this place
      a body lightened and sweetened
          and ready to be lifted up
      Strange to speak of the body in this way
          by my spirit has already fled
          and I am, even now, free to begin
          my new calling:
              to cultivate the ways of love
              and to teach the art of dying

THE SUNFLOWER

One relatively perfect sunflower,
tongues of snow and a lemon heart,
transplanted east-by-northeast off the lower porch,
no longer poised to take the sun because the house,
like a greedy billboard,
buys time and space
and the freedom of the light for over half the day,
twists head and shoulders round the porch
      like a velvet swan
and with wry neck and unembarrassed thirst,
drinks in the sun.

Emily Steward Shapcote

Emily Mary Gordon Steward was born in Liverpool, England in 1828. In 1856 she married the Reverend Edward Gifford Shapcote, an Anglican clergyman. In 1864 she accompanied her husband to his missionary assignment in South Africa, where their two sons were born. While there Mrs. Shapcote coverted to Roman Catholicism and, when the couple returned to England in 1868, her husband followed her. At a later date Emily Shapcote became a Dominican tertiary. Edward Shapcote later became assistant editor of the Catholic newspaper, *The Tablet*. Emily Shapcote was best known as a composer and lyricist of hymns, but she did produce three volumes of poetry. Her poems are mostly doctrinal and devotional. The Shapcotes' elder son, Edward Laurence, became a Dominican priest who worked on the English translation of *The Summa Theologica*. Like his parents, Father Shapcote served as a missionary in South Africa. Emily Shapcote died in 1909 in Stoneham, Devon, England.

MARY, THE PERFECT WOMAN

Prologue to Part One

I sing the song of songs, the song of love,
Which angels clad in glory may not sing.
I sing the inconceivable conceived,
The uncreated majesty of God
Cradling Himself upon the lap of times,
A creature –
                       In that vision I adore
The eye omnipotent, omniscience
Gazing upon the sweetness and the worth
Of one most beautiful conception.

                        He
Who in the form of humankind would be
Received into creation, then beheld,
When the worlds were not, the gracious entity
Of her whom He ordained His own to make
Above all other creatures – fair without,
Glorious within; saved from a shipwrecked race;
And graciously conceived in justice.
                        Then
The faultless image of Himself He viewed,
And loved supremely from eternity.

Acknowledgements

Our gratitude to the following for their kind permissions to reprint poems:

Dominican Province of England for the poems of Fathers Damian Magrath, O.P. and Vincent McNabb, O.P.;
Dominican Province of Saint Albert the Great for the poems of Father Benedict Ashley, O.P.;
Dominican Province of Saint Joseph for the poems of Fathers George Leonard Cochran, O.P., Thomas Heath, O.P. and Dominic Rover, O.P.;
Dominican Sisters of Adrian, Michigan for the poems of Sister Mary Jean Dorcy, O.P., copyright "Adrian Dominican Sisters; "

Dominican Sisters of Peace, Columbus, Ohio for the poems of Sister Maryanna Childs, O.P.;

Dominican Sisters of Sinsinawa, Wisconsin for the poems of Sister Mary Jeremy Finnegan, O.P.;

University of Detroit Press for the poems, *The Encounter* and *Out of the Ash,* by Brother Antoninus Everson, O.P., reprinted from *Crooked Lines of God* (pp. 60 and 88 respectively), 1959;

Sister Elizabeth Michael Boyle, O.P.;

Father Armando P. Ibáñez, O.P.;

Father Paul Murray, O.P.;

Father Christopher Renz, O.P.

All other poems are assumed to be in the public domain.

Credits

Drawings by Rev. Pere Hyacinth Besson, O.P. (1816-1861) and Rev. Pere Antonin Danzas, O.P. (1817-1861).

Photograph of Father Powell by Ashley Daubenmire McCabe.

Compiler and Editor

Matthew Donald Powell, O.P. was born in Springfield, Ohio into an Italian-American family, the original family name being *Paoletti*. Father Powell, a Dominican friar of the Province of Saint Joseph, has taught speech, theatre and English at the high school and college levels for more than thirty-five years. He earned an M.A. at Miami University (Ohio) and a Ph.D. from the University of Wisconsin at Madison. Father Powell previously served at Urbana University (Ohio), Tulane University (Louisiana) and Edgewood College (Wisconsin). Since 1983 he has taught theatre and English at Providence College in Rhode Island where he has specialized in history of the theatre, dramatic literature and the oral interpretation of poetry. He also served for eight years as chairman of the theatre department and directed plays by Peter Shaffer, George Bernard Shaw, Oscar Wilde, Thornton Wilder and Tennessee Williams. Father Powell is the author of five other books including *The Christmas Creche* and *God Off-Broadway: The Blackfriars Theatre*. He has had more than a dozen short stories published in magazines in the United States, Canada and Ireland. In addition, his short dramatizations are available from hitplays.com and havescripts.com. In 1998 and 2005 his work was recognized by the Catholic Press Association. Father Powell considers himself blessed to have lived in community with three of the poets included in this anthology: Fathers Ashley, Cochran and Rover.

Made in the USA
San Bernardino, CA
22 June 2018